Deborah!

May your & experiences fill you with purpose!

Sarah Clark

166 DAYS

MY JOURNEY THROUGH THE DARKNESS

JENNIFER CLARK

outskirtspress
DENVER, COLORADO

The opinions expressed in this manuscript are solely the opinions of the author and do not represent the opinions or thoughts of the publisher. The author has represented and warranted full ownership and/or legal right to publish all the materials in this book.

166 Days
My Journey Through The Darkness
All Rights Reserved.
Copyright © 2014 Jennifer Clark
v3.0

Cover Photo © 2014 Jennifer Clark. All rights reserved - used with permission.

This book may not be reproduced, transmitted, or stored in whole or in part by any means, including graphic, electronic, or mechanical without the express written consent of the publisher except in the case of brief quotations embodied in critical articles and reviews.

Outskirts Press, Inc.
http://www.outskirtspress.com

ISBN: 978-1-4787-2332-5

Outskirts Press and the "OP" logo are trademarks belonging to Outskirts Press, Inc.

PRINTED IN THE UNITED STATES OF AMERICA

This book is dedicated to my friends and family whose love and support carried through my time in Afghanistan.

To Tera….thank you for being my flashlight.

Becky, I love you so much and thank God it was you by my side. Friends for life.

To my Gerg….there are no words…you are my soul. Without you I would have no purpose.

To my children. May you always see the beauty through the darkness and have the strength and courage to find the meaning in the life circumstances that you cannot understand.

To anyone out there who is going through something and needs hope to help them get through it….My story is for you.

Contents

Part One

Chapter 1
    Who is this Woman?.. 1
Chapter 2
    Almost Two Years Earlier…Leaving Home 4
    Day 1: Boots on the Ground 18
    Day 2: Waiting 21
    Day 3: We have a flight 31
Chapter 3
    Day 4: Saying Hello to Bagram Air Field 33
Chapter 4
    Day 5: The Flashing Light.. 37
Chapter 5
    Day 6: Medic Warriors 39
Chapter 6
    Day 7: How Bazaar 44
Chapter 7
    Day 14: Salute to a Fallen Comrade... 46
Chapter 8
    Day 19: One Year Later.. 49
Chapter 9
    Day 28: Final Destination Revealed... 53
Chapter 10
    Days 32 and 33: One of Our Own 56

Chapter 11
    Day 37: Here We Go 60
Chapter 12
    Day 44: The "No Limit" Soldier Has Limits 64
Chapter 13
    Day 45: Preparing to Go 71
Chapter 14
    Days 47 & 48: The MedCap 76
Chapter 15
    Day 49: Happy Anniversary 89
Chapter 16
    Days 53-57: Working with the FST 91
Chapter 17
    Day 58: Arrival at the Firebase 96
Chapter 18
    Day 59: First Taste of War 103
Chapter 19
    Day 62: Settling In 109
Chapter 20
    Day 63: Casualties of War 111
    Day 66: Independence Day 116
Chapter 21
    Day 67: Another Year Older 118
Chapter 22
    Day 72: Touching Hands 120
    Day 76: Similarities across Oceans 124
Chapter 23
    Day 77: Missing My Gerg 138
Chapter 24
    Days 80-86: Divine Intervention 140
Chapter 25
    Days 87-88: Close Encounters of the Taliban Kind 142
Chapter 26
    Day 93: A Different Kind of Wounded Warrior 148
Chapter 27
    Day 98: The Best I Could Do 151
Chapter 28
    Day 104: The Little Big Things 155

Chapter 29
    Day 106: Out of my Hands.. 158
    Days 107-111: A Father's Struggle.. 163
Chapter 30
    Day 112: Reality Check 165
Chapter 31
    Day 113: A Day in the Life of a Green Beret 168
Chapter 32
    Days 116-117: My War Within 174
Chapter 33
    Day 121: Running for my Sanity 178
Chapter 34
    Days 126-127: The Worst Day of My Life............................ 182
Chapter 35
    Day 129: My Grieving 197
Chapter 36
    Day 132: New Hope 199
Chapter 37
    Day 134: Shut Down 203
Chapter 38
    Day 135: 9/11 205
Chapter 39
    Day 142: Falling Apart.. 207
Chapter 40
    Day 144: Leaving Hell 212
Chapter 41
    Day 145: Back to Reality 215
Chapter 42
    Days 148-161: Back to Bagram 219
Chapter 43
    Days 162-166: The Journey Home 224

Part Two

Chapter 44
    The Aftermath 231
Chapter 45
    Back to Center 246

PART ONE

CHAPTER 1

Who is this Woman?

6 December 2009

Tonight I realized I was in serious trouble. After fourteen months of suppressing any emotion that reminded me of that horrible time, I finally reached the point of no return. I rolled over in bed, exhausted from the previous two sleepless nights. I looked up at my alarm clock and saw it was 12:00 am. My tiny newborn daughter was screaming in hunger from her bassinet at the foot of my bed. I dragged my tired body of out bed and picked up Ayla and cradled her in my arms. My new angel was such an amazing little person already and I was so grateful to have her in my life. She was my whole world; my love for her was incredible. I knew this love would make all the hurt I was trying so desperately not to feel go away. It had to. I had come to where I didn't know what else to do to avoid going "there" and she had become my reason to move on.

I wanted to do everything by the books and be the best mom I could for her, so I was adamant about breastfeeding. She was born three weeks early and we had struggled with this in the hospital, but I was determined. I sat down with her in my bed and began to try to feed her. She continued to cry.

"Ok, Jenn…be patient, you can do this," I told myself, "Remember the different methods they taught you in the hospital." I thought about the endless piles of paperwork they gave me when they discharged us two days before and tried to use the recommendations. Unfortunately, I had no luck. Her screams became louder.

I have to do this! I thought. *Why can't she just do what the books say?* I felt my emotions bubbling under the surface; a situation that had become such a norm for me over the last several months since I returned from Afghanistan. I had mastered the art of avoidance; keeping all of my pain at arm's length by dodging anything that reminded me of what I had been through.

Now she was screaming. *Oh my God, I don't know what the hell to do!* I was losing my composure. I looked at the clock again, 2:00am. Two hours had disappeared into the night and I was still in the same place I was when we started. Her screams became louder and her little voice was becoming hoarse.

My Physician Assistant instincts kicked in. *What if she is dehydrated?* I thought. I reached down and put my finger on her tongue; it was dry. *Oh, my God! She is!* I looked down at her with concern... but I didn't see Ayla. I was holding *that* baby - the dying baby in Afghanistan. Her brother had carried her into my clinic in what looked like a potato sack draped over his shoulder, plopped her down on my gurney and untied his sack. I looked inside and saw the skin and bones of what used to be a healthy baby girl, now minutes from death. There was nothing that I could do to save her. As I looked down at my daughter I was right back there, in that horrible place. I could smell the filth in the air and I could hear the breaths slowly leaving the baby girl's tiny, dying body.

I snapped. "Greg! Wake up!" I screamed at my husband as he lay next to me completely oblivious to my rapid descent into panic.

"What is it, Jenn? What's wrong? Is Ayla ok?" He jumped out of bed braced for the worst.

"She's starving! I can't feed her! She's dehydrated, look at her!" I screamed.

"Calm down, sweetie. It's okay," he tried.

"No! It's not ok! Please! Do something! Please Greg! Go to the store and buy some formula, look at her!" I pleaded.

"She's ok, don't worry! Remember they gave us some samples at the hospital? I'll go fix a bottle." He rushed to the kitchen and returned shortly with a bottle in hand. "Here, I'll take her," he said, and finally our screaming baby was content.

Alone in bed, I began to cry. I realized what had just happened, my first flashback. This thing was real. I was not ok. I was damaged goods, and I didn't know how to fix it. I knew the deployment would change me, but I had no idea that *this* is who would come back from it. Who had I become? The once joyful, funny, optimistic person who had everything under control was lost and nowhere to be found; instead this damaged, emotional wreck had taken over.

I thought about Ayla. Her name had been predetermined for many years; Ayla, after a strong female character in the novel <u>Clan of the Cave Bear</u> that was passed down through the generations of women in my family. The story illustrated a young lady, who despite all odds grew into an amazing woman of strength and character. Her middle name Lee was in honor of my grandmother who was such an influence for me growing up. I had thought I was going to be that strong influence for my daughter, but now I had no idea who I was anymore. My little girl would never know who I once had been. I knew the deployment would be a major part of my life, so I kept a journal to document that time in my life for my future children. Now that child was here; what would she think of her mother?

How had I come to this point? I thought of the journal. It held the key to who I was and who I had become. It was the story of how my life changed forever due to the most traumatic experience I'd ever endured. That night I knew what I had to do…I had to relive it, in its entirety, if I had any hope of rescuing the lost soul inside of me.

CHAPTER **2**

Almost Two Years Earlier... Leaving Home

24 April 2008

It had finally come. After all the preparation time, anticipation, and dread, the day had arrived. I felt so overwhelmed with every emotion possible that I was beside myself as I sat in the terminal waiting to board the plane out of Panama City. I showed up at the airport in civilian clothes, and once I got there I saw another Air Force member in uniform. Greg saw me looking at him and I blurted out, "Greg! I should go change...I knew I should've worn my uniform. I am going to look so stupid being the only one showing up in civvies!"

"Jenn, no you're not. You're fine; you don't need to put on your uniform until you're leaving the country. You know that. Relax, dork!"

I was so nervous. Neither one of us wanted to prolong the goodbye, knowing it would make it that much harder. So we quickly hugged and gave each other a kiss and that was it. Typical of me, I let my nerves get the best of me, and as soon as he left I rushed to the bathroom and changed into uniform, despite his advice. I had never done anything like this before, and it was so blatantly obvious by my actions. I was traveling from Panama City to Norfolk, VA where I would fly out the next day to begin my journey to Afghanistan. This was my first deployment after being in the Air Force for almost eight years.

ALMOST TWO YEARS EARLIER...LEAVING HOME

When I said goodbye to my Greg that day, I couldn't help but realize I was saying goodbye to the life I had known up until that day. I knew without a doubt this experience would change my life in many ways, and I hoped that change would be all in a positive light. I was scared to death and excited all at once for what I was about to do.

After being stationed at Tyndall AFB for just under a year, my squadron commander called me into his office one morning to inform me I had a deployment tasking. I would be going to Afghanistan for six months. My orders were very vague, so vague, in fact, that no one at Tyndall even knew what I would be doing once I arrived. At one point I was told I would be working with the "female detainees" at the prison at Bagram Airfield. Through networking and research I was able to make contact with the PA I was replacing. I emailed her so many questions; "Can you tell me about the female detainees? What type of working conditions should I expect? What are the most common ailments you see?"

Her response was not what I was expecting. "Jennifer, I am sorry to tell you this, but there are no female *detainees*. You are not going to work at the prison. They didn't tell you that you would be outside the wire?"

Um...no! They did not! I thought to myself as I read her words.

"You will be attached to a team of Green Berets at a firebase, running the clinic there, meaning you will be treating the locals and the team."

My jaw dropped. *Oh my God.*

She continued, "I am sorry you didn't have these details. I am happy to help with whatever information I can. You need to prepare yourself to see a lot of trauma. This is not the medicine we are used to practicing back home."

Her words jumped off the computer screen and became entangled in my emotion. *Green Berets. Outside the wire. Local nationals. Trauma. Danger. War. I'm not prepared. Oh my God. Combat.*

As one might imagine, I experienced many emotions upon receiving this news; fear, sadness, excitement, disbelief, surprise to name a few. Greg and I had many long discussions anticipating what was in store for me. We often laughed at the irony of the situation: I had tried to dump him several years before over the "idea" of his wanting to be involved with Special Forces when he was active duty, and now I was the one getting *all kinds* of involved with them, in Afghanistan of all places.

I had always had an urge to do humanitarian medicine, and it certainly sounded as though that was exactly what I would be doing. I knew it would be scary, sad, beautiful, heartwarming, and chilling all at once. Admittedly, up until that point in my life, I was a very "innocent" person when it came to what I had seen and done in my career. I was a brand new Physician Assistant and a brand new military officer, with just under a year of experience in both. Understandably, the majority of the time I felt completely out of my league with many of the things I had to do on a day-to-day basis. I didn't have much of a backbone for no other reason than the fact that I had little to no experience to back my decisions. I hoped I would be able to grow that backbone quickly where I was going.

It was so hard to say goodbye... to everyone. You don't realize the impact people have on your life until you are in a situation where you are completely alone. I was the only person I'd have to lean on for the next six months.

As I sat in the terminal in my newly donned uniform, I watched the other Air Force guy pass through security. His eyes scanned the crowd and he locked eyes with me and smiled at the familiar face in uniform and sat down beside me. "How are you doing, Ma'am?" he asked.

"I'm fine; how are you?" I replied. We began to talk about where we were heading. I told him my story and he told me his; he was off to Virginia as well for training and a possible deployment.

And then he said it. "Man, I wish I could change. The only reason I'm in uniform is because I came straight from work and didn't have time to change clothes."

What!? I felt like a complete idiot! I had managed to force myself into flying in my uncomfortable uniform for no other reason than letting

ALMOST TWO YEARS EARLIER...LEAVING HOME

myself overanalyze the situation and let my nerves get the best of me. Oh well! I laughed to myself thinking about what Greg would say.

"Yeah, I know what you mean," I lied. What an idiot I was! The attendant called for my boarding group and I quickly gathered my things, wished him well, and boarded the plane. I found my seat by the window. As the wheels left the safe and familiar asphalt of the Panama City runway, tears streamed down my face. I realized that I wouldn't see this place again for six long months. I watched the city slowly fade away in the clouds and pulled myself together thinking, *I am in this now*.

Once we landed in Atlanta, I made it off the plane without any complications and successfully found the connection gate. As I was waiting to board, I looked around and noticed many other military personnel. They were not in uniform, of course, but I could tell by their haircuts and demeanors they were in the service as well. I was the only one in uniform, and that was very apparent. I felt even more uncomfortable as the moments passed, but that was not the end of it. As we were getting ready for take-off, the flight attendant grabbed the intercom and began her standard preflight instructions of exit rows, oxygen masks, etc. So naturally I began to lose myself in my newly found addiction of Sudoku.

Then I heard it: "Attention ladies and gentlemen, we have a VIP on board with us today! I would like to bring your attention to our *only* uniformed soldier, Lt. Clark, sitting in the back of the plane. Let's give her a round of applause and thank her for her service."

My face turned every shade of red possible, especially knowing that there were at least ten other military members on board who were smart enough to stay in their civilian clothes. They were undoubtedly getting a laugh out of my situation. Honestly, I couldn't help but chuckle at it myself. I could just imagine what Greg would say. I decided not to even try to guess how many "I told you so's" would come flowing from his mouth. It was the very first travel day, and I was already pulling out the "Jenisms".

25 April 2008

In Norfolk, VA I had my last dirty martini for six months with my friend Tony. I met him at Advanced Contingency Skills Training (ACST), a combat skills course that we had to complete prior to the deployment. He was a Logistics officer, who as luck would have it, would most likely be in charge of the logistical needs of my unit. This meant he would be able to secure flights in between the forward operating bases (FOBs) which was a much better mode of travel than the alternative of vehicle convoys. He had also been very helpful with my out-processing from Tyndall AFB. No one there seemed to know what was going on with my deployment, but Tony had much more insight into the system and his advice made it as smooth as possible for me. That being said, it was still a logistical nightmare to actually get to the point where I was. If I hadn't read the fine print on my orders and out-processing checklist as carefully as I did, Lord knows what would have happened to me. As we sat and ate dinner looking out over the water I said, "Tony, I just want to thank you again for your help during my out-processing. It was really nice to have some support."

"Jenn, no biggy; that's what we do. We take care of each other. I promise to continue to help in whatever ways I can," he said.

"Thank you" I said.

Our rotator flight was scheduled to leave that night at 2030 hours. We were scheduled to make several stops in Canada, Iceland, Budapest, and The Republic of Georgia, ultimately landing in Manas, Kyrgyzstan where we would likely be for several days until we could get a flight out to Bagram Airfield. Manas is in the Area of Operational Readiness (AOR) and from what I had been told, once we touched ground there, the deployment would officially start.

26 April 2008

After stopping in Newfoundland and Iceland I found myself sitting in the airport in Budapest, Hungary; it'd been a long trip. We had one more scheduled stop in Georgia before Manas. It had been so interesting stopping in several countries. We were there for such

ALMOST TWO YEARS EARLIER...LEAVING HOME

short periods of time, but still got a small glimpse of their cultures by having some interactions with the people at the airports. Such a minimal exposure to different cultures gave me new insight into many things and I found myself longing to know more. In Iceland (probably the most barren and desolate-looking place I had ever seen) the people actually still spoke the language of the Vikings! I noted that, at the time, the American dollar was not worth much in any of the places we stopped. I'd found the same thing to be true when Greg and I went to Ireland just prior to my departure, and I discovered the mighty Euro.

Seeing these places made me think of the deployment. Now that I was on my way, parts of me were actually excited. For many years I had dreamed of being able to practice humanitarian medicine and now I had an opportunity to live it. I thought of all the people I would be able to help and I smiled. I was going to make a real difference for these people; what an honor. I knew there would be dangerous parts of it, but I just knew the people I would treat would make it all worth the risk.

27 April 2008

At 0300 hours we finally made it to the last stop before Manas... Georgia. We were on the ground for approximately one and a half hours but were unable to go into the terminal due to security reasons. We were thankful to at least be able to deplane and stretch our legs on the runway while the plane refueled.

It felt surreal as I stood on the tarmac in Georgia, under a large full moon gazing into a sea of the silhouettes of two hundred soldiers and airmen on the verge of entering the war. Some were so young and inexperienced; no more than eighteen years old, while others showed signs of age and experience through their grey hairs and determined eyes. I had to ask myself where in this continuum of knowledge and experience I fell. I was older than most of the young soldiers, and had experience from my eight years of enlisted service, but I felt I was glowing a fluorescent "green" when it came to my understanding of what it took to be an officer and a leader, so much so that it felt eerily similar to how I felt the day I got off the bus at Lackland AFB for my first day of Basic Military Training. I concluded I fit somewhere in the middle.

Seeing such young troops surround me made me reflect on my own life. I joined the Air Force when I was twenty years old in August 2000. I was a sophomore in college at Fort Hays State University in Hays, KS and had come to find myself lost without a passion, a very uncomfortable feeling for someone who thought she had it all figured out. When I went to college, I had a scholarship for broadcasting, with every intention of becoming the next Barbara Walters, but when I started taking the classes I realized very quickly that Barbara and I were just not going to have that connection. The industry was not what I thought it was; therefore, as time went on, I felt increasingly confused, having been so sure about my choice of a major when I graduated from high school.

Disappointment was an understatement. I was now that young person I once felt "sorry" for as the wise and all-knowing eighteen-year-old that I was. Once confident that I had it all figured out, now I had no idea what I wanted to be when I grew up….and I was scared. Around the time of this newly acquired humility I enrolled in a biology course. I had an amazing professor who was passionate about her field, and I quickly came to realize I was falling in love with the study of life and began to feel a sense of hope in finding my new career path. I started to research avenues I could take, and healthcare became the missing puzzle piece.

Around the time of this personal epiphany I met Will, a boy I dated, and our short time together changed my life forever. He was an Air Force brat, and in many conversations he would tell me how he felt I should be an officer in the USAF. I thought that was absolutely ridiculous and I would laugh saying "Yeah! Right! *Me?* Do you even know who you are talking to? *No thank you.*"

Again, I obviously knew everything, after all, I was eighteen. Interestingly though, something happened; the more he persisted the

ALMOST TWO YEARS EARLIER...LEAVING HOME

more open to the idea I became. I began to see what an opportunity it actually was. Several months later Will and I broke up and I was devastated. I found myself picking up the pieces to my life. I had lost my major. I was brokenhearted and emotionally lost, due to all that I had invested in the relationship. Then, one day of many that I was immersed in feeling sorry for myself, I opened the USAF website, clicked on the link to request more information, and the next thing I knew I was on a bus to basic training in San Antonio, TX. I got selected for a job as an Air Force medic, so after I completed basic training I went through technical school to learn the skills of a nurse assistant and EMT-Basic.

I got my focus back. I was eager to gain as much knowledge as I could from my military experience with plans to finish college and get commissioned as some sort of medical officer. Life was good again. After tech school, I was stationed at Nellis AFB in Las Vegas, Nevada and my first assignment was working on the medical surgical (Med/Surg) floor. I was responsible for all of the not-so-fun tasks like bathing the patients, dressing changes, cleaning bedside commodes, etc. Even doing this work I realized I had a passion for taking care of people. On night shift, once all my duties were complete, instead of sitting at the nurse's station shooting the breeze, I would often find myself in with the patients listening to their stories when no one else would; I met some of the most amazing individuals whom I would never forget.

My favorite conversations were with the World War II vets. I had a special place in my heart for them due to the fact my grandfather was a 1st Lieutenant in WWII. I always wished I could have heard him describe his experience, but unfortunately he died when I was only nine years old. I remember growing up, my grandmother used to tell me when he came home after being at war for four years, he sat down with her and told her, "You can ask me about it this once, and then we will never talk about it again." I never understood that as a child.

Time went on and after a year on the Med/Surg floor I was transferred to the Surgery Clinic. While working there I was able to return to school and complete my Associates degree in Allied Health Sciences through the Community College of the Air Force. I had big plans; my feeling of having it all figured out returned, except this time it was "for real". I decided to finish my Bachelor's degree in nursing through an Air Force commissioning program that would allow me to go to school full time for the remaining two years of school I had left. After completing my nursing degree, I planned to go on and become a physical therapist. I had the perfect plan and I was well on my way to my goal by working closely with the base education office, my commanders and mentors; their feedback was encouraging. Based on my military awards and GPA I was led to believe I was a shoo-in for the nursing program. I was certain everything was happening the way it was supposed to. My package was submitted, and it became a waiting game.

While I was working in the Surgery clinic I met a Physician Assistant student. Up until that point I had no idea what a PA was. The student explained that PAs were mid-level providers who could evaluate and treat patients in a very similar way to doctors, but a doctor was responsible for being a preceptor for their work. It was a Master's degree and one of the fastest growing career fields at the time.

As I listened to him tell me about it, I realized what an amazing way to impact the lives of patients it could be and began to love the idea of it. I could make a much bigger difference for the patients and their families I had grown to love than I could in my current position. I remember telling Greg, "I kind of hope my package gets denied, then maybe I'll look into this PA thing instead."

Several weeks later I got the notification I had been waiting for; the board had met, decisions had been made for who was accepted into the nursing program. As I opened my email, I was already celebrating my selection…and then….I saw it….the word that took the wind out of my nursing school sails: *Disqualified*.

What??! Disqualified? How could that be? I was beyond upset, I was *devastated*. I just *knew* I would be accepted. I had looked over my package with a fine-tooth comb. I did everything that was

ALMOST TWO YEARS EARLIER...LEAVING HOME

required, and I had exceeded all of the standards. My commanders and supervisors were equally shocked. I could tell they felt horrible for falsely leading such a young airman to believe she was invincible. I went home that day and cried and cried on Greg's shoulder. I was so upset with God. I felt I was being prevented from doing absolutely what was meant for me to do.

The next day I opened the email again and called the provided contact phone number to find out what had disqualified what everyone thought was the "perfect package." The reason left me speechless. The base education office didn't sign my cover letter, so as soon as it made it to the board, it wasn't even opened. The very first page stopped them from going any further. I couldn't wrap my head around it. I remember going home that evening, sitting in silence, soaking it in, trying to find the reason, and having a very loud conversation with God about how I felt about the whole thing.

"I don't understand," I pleaded, "I felt so sure you were guiding me down this path, for what? Only to fail? I feel like such an idiot. Now I have to face everyone and their disappointment!" I was so embarrassed at my certainty of acceptance. "God, you and I go way back. Surely there is a very important reason for this, *right?*" The next day I felt reassured that the reason for the circumstances would come to light eventually.

As time passed, I looked more seriously at the idea of being a PA. The more I researched, the more I felt it was worth pursuing. After a year in the Surgery clinic, I was transferred to the Emergency Room, and I loved every minute of it. I had the opportunity to work closely with many doctors and PAs, and was able to hone my skills as an EMT. My love of my patients continued to grow with me through my experiences. While the pace of the ER was much quicker than the Med/Surg floor or the Surgery clinic, I continued to spend time with patients, listening to their stories.

I will never forget one night an elderly man came in with chest pain. He was all alone, and I could tell he was beyond scared. He was lost in a sea of wires, IV tubing, EKGs, the portable x-ray machine, doctors, nurses, and me. Initially, of course, we rushed his bed and got all of the necessary labs, x-rays, and medications on board, and then he was all alone again, waiting for the answer to what was happening to him, which could very well affect the rest of his life. As he waited for what probably seemed like an eternity, he had no other option but to listen to us as we referred to our patients as bed numbers. He happened to be "Bed 2".

When things calmed down, I found myself drawn to his bedside. I pulled up a stool, held his hand and said, "Sir, don't worry; everything is going to be ok." He started talking, and before we knew it we were having an amazing conversation about his time in Japan in World War II. He talked about several of the missions he was on; I listened in amazement at what he had been through.

He came to a point where he just stared off into space, and we sat in silence. He finally spoke again. "You know, kid, I gotta tell you, back then, going into battle knowing damn well what I was facing, having to fire my weapon on someone else and possibly not surviving - that was nothing compared to how scared I am right now." I wished so much I could take his fear away. I squeezed his hand and began talking to him about meaningless things to get his mind off of the unknown.

Several hours later he was admitted, and as they wheeled him off to the elevator, he grabbed my hand and squeezed. "Thank you" were the last words he spoke to me. Once he disappeared into the elevator, I never saw him again.

I felt a sense of fulfillment in the Emergency Room; I was growing up, meanwhile still pursuing becoming a PA. I completed the required classes, submitted my package and nervously awaited the results. I was an E-4 with a line number for an E-5, with only three and a half years of military experience; the odds were certainly against me. The average person who was selected at that time had over ten years of military experience, average rank was E-6 and above. I knew despite my grades, military record and my recommendations, it was a long shot. Several months went by and then finally the results were in. I

ALMOST TWO YEARS EARLIER...LEAVING HOME

couldn't bear it! What would the answer be? Would it be another disappointment? Another disqualification? I damn well knew my cover letter was signed, that was for sure!

I could feel my heart beating out of my chest as I opened the email. I scrolled down through what seemed like a never-ending list of eighteen names; and then to my amazement, I saw my name! I was overjoyed with excitement. I couldn't wait to tell Greg, and that evening when I did he chuckled and said, "Aren't you glad you didn't get that cover letter signed last time?" I was informed of my selection in 2004, and my class didn't start until the following May in 2005.

Over the next year I put on SSgt (E-5) and continued working in the Emergency Room and going to school. In May, 2005 I relocated to San Antonio and began the most intense schooling I had ever experienced. We completed one hundred credit hours that first year. My class census was just over sixty people when we started, by graduation we had lost over half of the students who started with us, due to wash-outs.

Despite the stress, I truly loved what I was learning. The program was called the Interservice Physician Assistant Program (IPAP) and was intended for service members from the Air Force, Army, Navy, and Coast Guard. We all spent the first year together at the campus at Fort Sam Houston for the didactic portion of the program, and the second year we would be sent to various bases to attend our clinical rotations based on our respective branch of service.

I loved my class; we had such a unique melting pot of personalities which made our long days together fun. A couple of my classmates were former Green Beret medics. I remember thinking what an odd sense of humor they had, sure that they really had a few "screws loose". I had no way to anticipate that in the very near future the Green Berets would bring me to know several men that I still consider brothers to this day.

My world was school for the next two years; I woke up at 0500, studied, and then went to class from 0730 to 1630. I got home and ate a quick dinner, took no more than an hour break and then resumed studying until I went to bed. When I woke in the morning my routine started all over again.

I graduated with my Bachelor's degree in the spring of 2006 and ironically was assigned back to Nellis AFB for my clinical rotations. It was incredible to come back to the same hospital I worked at as a young medic, now as a PA student interacting with the providers I had known before in such a different way. After completing my year of clinicals, in May, 2007 I received my Master's Degree in Physician Assistant Studies, and I was commissioned.

During the ceremony I was able to choose who would pin my bars on, and undoubtedly it was Greg. He had sacrificed so much for that day to happen, so of course it was his place. That moment was so special to me. My mother gave me my grandfather's Lieutenant Bars that he wore in WWII, and as Greg pinned them on, I felt such a connection to my grandfather, knowing he was somewhere smiling down on me. I was twenty-six years old, standing in front of my family and colleagues and officially 1st Lieutenant Jennifer Clark; a moment that was surreal. After the crazy road of disappointment I had been traveling on for so many years, it was hard to believe I'd really accomplished the goal I had set, and I was actually a PA and an officer. I had made it to SSgt as an enlisted medic, and had learned so much from my experiences as an enlisted airman. I was so proud to have been prior enlisted; I vowed that day that I would be the best officer I could be, ensuring I would never lose sight of the importance of what the enlisted members of the military do every day.

I will never forget my first day of seeing patients as an official PA. I was so nervous that I would make a mistake, I was beside myself. I studied my schedule the night before and re-read everything I could possibly find in my textbooks about the diagnoses the patients were scheduled to be seen for. I had to know any and every scenario that could present. Greg and his reassuring hugs and tough love helped carry me through the initial days. He had a great way of telling me to suck it up, put on my big girl panties and get over it! Yet, when I

ALMOST TWO YEARS EARLIER...LEAVING HOME

needed his softer side, he was there. How quickly time had passed, so much seemed to happen in my life in a few short years.

Tony nudged my arm. "Hey, Jenn! Let's go!"
"Huh?" I replied, realizing I had been lost in my memories.
"You ready?" he asked. "They're calling us to re-board the plane."
"Oh, ok. Yeah, let's go." I looked up at the moon again, took a deep breath and headed back to the aircraft. Tony and I sat together the majority of the trip, and after many hours of training and flight time together he had a clear understanding of what I would be doing once we arrived.

As we prepared for takeoff, he leaned over and said to me, "Hey, I've been thinking about what you've told me you'll be doing on this deployment."

"Really? What about it?" I asked.

"Just remember, Jenn, if you get into trouble out there, *run*. Don't try to be a hero," he answered. As I heard him speak those words I began to wonder, *what would I do if something horrible did happen*? I had never been in a situation like that, and I couldn't say I knew how I would act. I knew how I *hoped* I would react, but I was well aware that how a person feels she would handle a situation is often different from the way she actually does. I recalled many times hearing of situations in which the most unlikely person performed heroic acts, or, on the contrary, the most qualified person to handle a tragedy couldn't take the pressure and cowered in the corner.

As I digested his statement and pondered the unknown, I prayed that I would never have to find the answer to the perplexing question of how I personally would react. I looked at the clock, Manas.....four hours away.....

Day 1
Boots on the Ground

27 April 2008

As we flew over Kyrgyzstan I could see the barren, mountainous earth below. "Ladies and gentlemen, we are now on our final descent into Manas. Please fasten your seatbelts and ensure your tray tables are in the upright position and your seatbacks are fully forward. It has been our pleasure and honor to serve you, the men and women of the Armed Forces on this flight. Please stay safe and come home soon."

The time had dragged for the past twenty seven hours of flight time, but all of a sudden it seemed to race by. The ground was coming closer and closer and then that familiar sensation of the wheels touching ground, and we were there. It was now an official deployment. "Here we go," is all I could manage to say with a smile to my fellow deployers, but inside my heart was pounding and my thoughts were racing.

Once we taxied to our stopping point on the tarmac another voice sounded over the intercom, only this time it was not the friendly flight attendant, but a harsh military voice telling us to "stand by" and wait for further instruction on deplaning. The voice called for the baggage detail to come forward to begin unloading all of our belongings. A mass of young enlisted troops from both the Army and Air Force plowed forward. Eventually, after the detail had secured our things, they gave us the okay to deplane. As my foot stepped off of the last stair, and onto the asphalt, I had a sudden change of mindset. I was now *in* this, boots on the ground, and it was time to toughen up and be a "soldier" for six months.

Luckily Tony's friend, Tim, who was also traveling with us, had a girlfriend (Tracy) who was conveniently deployed to Manas as the commander of the Security Forces squadron and was waiting for us on the flight line with her pickup truck. She greeted us with a smile. "It's great to see you all made it," she said as she waited while we got our bags loaded into the bed of the truck. After we secured all of our belongings she was gracious enough to give us a tour of the base. As we drove, she explained where everything was and the basics on how the base operated.

"So this place is pretty small, but easy to navigate," she stated. "All of the transient tents, where people are typically required to stay, are off to your left; but not to worry, I have secured rooms for you all tonight with some permanent party troops. Jenn, you can stay with me."

"Wow, thank you so much," I said gratefully. The transient tents could've easily been a disaster; an open bay, sleeping on cots and nights filled with hopes that no one would steal our stuff. Her room was very small, but we could both fit reasonably comfortably and I was thankful for her gracious offer.

She eventually pulled up to the Personnel Command (PERSCO) tent, which was where we in-processed the base. She dropped us off and said, "I'll come back to pick you guys up after the briefing."

We surrendered our ID cards and waited in typical military fashion to be told what to do next. The PERSCO members explained that we were to stay in the transient tents (thankfully we would not).

"While you are required to keep accountability of your weapons at all times, you are not required to wear them on your person. This means someone has to be in the presence of the weapon at all times," said the airman giving us the briefing. This made sense with all that we had been trained prior to leaving country. He continued, "The linens for your cots are in the building across the street on the right. In order to obtain your sheets and pillow you will be required to present two copies of your orders. You are all considered on stand-by status for the next available flight to your final destinations. This means you will need to check in with the terminal every eight hours to see if you are listed on the manifest for the next flight out. Does anyone have any questions?" We all sat in silence, waiting to be dismissed.

After the briefing, Tracy returned and picked us up as promised with a wonderful surprise. "Great news, guys," she said. "I've arranged for you to store your weapons at the Armory." In that moment I decided she was my new best friend. She had done so much to help make our time there as comfortable as possible.

The rest of the day was spent getting settled, going to the gym and running off the past twenty seven hours of plane time, and finally catching up on sleep. It was Day One of what I expected to be a very unique and life-changing experience.

Day 2
Waiting

28 April 2008

We woke up early in morning, ate breakfast and went straight to the terminal to see if we had a flight out to Bagram; disappointingly we discovered there was nothing. Instead, we saw our names on a list with a big fat "pending" beside them, which meant later, rather than sooner, on getting out of there. We all looked at each other thinking, *So now what?* We decided to check out the base amenities and stumbled across a wonderful perk of being in the AOR, we could get a full body massage for one full hour for only....are you ready?.... $20! What a great deal! I scheduled myself one of those ASAP. I tended to carry a lot of my stress in my back and I paid for it; I was constantly plagued with knots that could become quite painful at times. My current situation certainly fell under the "high stress" category. With my massage scheduled, I realized I needed a phone and wireless internet so I could contact everyone; especially my husband. It was midday in Manas; therefore, it was in the middle of the night back home, which meant I needed to wait to call until later on in the evening. They offered morale phone calls, which were free, but they were limited to only fifteen minutes a call and we could only use them twice a week. Fortunately, they also had a café with wireless internet and phones where people could pay a small fee to use if they chose.

We decided to go for a run and workout to kill some more time. After we finished the workout we were walking around the base and as I looked up I saw a very familiar appearing face in a crowd of people. It was Dwight, a friend of mine from when I was enlisted; we had gone to technical school together when I was learning how to be a medic nearly eight years prior and hadn't seen each other since.

"Oh my gosh! Dwight! I can't believe it's you! Of all places to have a reunion!"

"Wow, Jenn, How are you?" he said.

"Doing awesome, I'm a PA now, and en route to Bagram. What about you?"

"A PA? Wow that's great! I'm so happy for you. I am actually stationed here for another three months. I'm working in the acute care clinic," he said. We stood around and chatted, catching up on each other's lives. He was newly married and permanently stationed in California. I had heard the expression "It's a small Air Force" for years, and that moment was my first experience when that statement was made true. We agreed to meet up later that evening at a place called "Pete's," a hangout spot where we could actually have up to two alcoholic drinks in a 24 hour period….that is, as long as you were not in the Army, and as luck would have it…I was in the Air Force, so a drink I would have!

After dinner we got issued our C-Bags, which were filled with our nuclear, biological, and chemical (NBC) gear and our Individual Body Armor. The bag was the heaviest thing I had ever lifted, so heavy in fact; I couldn't walk more than five steps with it before I had to rest. It quite possibly weighed at least, if not more, than what I did.

"Jenn, are you ok? Do you need some help with that?" Tony asked.

"No!" I insisted. "I've got it. I just need to stop here and there for a break."

He looked at me and shook his head. "Stubborn!" he said as he stood waiting as I insistently struggled with my bag. He was right, the last thing I needed was someone to do it for me, even though I secretly would have loved to hand it over. After what seemed like miles of carrying the bag, and my pride, I was thankful to drop it off at the terminal and head on to Pete's. We all sat around talking for a while and I continued to catch up with Dwight about what was happening in our lives. It was nice to see an old friend, but the whole time we were there I was constantly checking my watch; waiting for a reasonable time to call Greg. After what felt like an eternity it was finally a decent time back home so I hurried to the phone and waited in line to talk to him. I waited for what seemed hours but in reality it was only a few minutes. I got to my booth and dialed his number. The first time I heard his voice the tears instantly welled up in my eyes and a huge lump formed in my throat.

"Hi," was all I could manage initially.

"Hi sweetie! How are you?" he asked. "It already seems like you have been gone for so long! How was the flight? Where are you?"

I told him the story about my uniform fiasco at the airport, and he laughed. "What did I tell you, Nej?" was all he could manage to say in between bouts of laughter.

I missed him so much already and my deployment was just getting started. We talked for about fifteen minutes and then we had to hang up. There was so much I wanted to say to him, but didn't have the chance. As I walked back to my room I smiled as I remembered the story of how we met.

April 18, 2003 I went to a country music bar on the strip in Las Vegas. I absolutely did not want to go out that night. I had every intention of cuddling up on my couch in my pajamas with a big bowl of popcorn and watching movies all night with my cat. My girlfriends; however, had different plans.

"Jenn! Come on! It'll be fun! We need a good night out on the town, just us girls! When was the last time we were all together and able to go dancing?" asked my friend Olivia.

"I'm not sure," was my response.

"You see? You have to go! We are long overdue for a girls' night!" After much persuasion they convinced me a night of country music and dancing was what I needed, so I reluctantly put my robe and slippers away and agreed to go. The whole way there I was regretting I let them talk me into putting up with the traffic, Las Vegas tourists, and loud music.

As soon as I walked in I went to the bar, sat down and ordered my favorite drink at the time; cranberry and vodka, and began trying to convince myself I was going to have a good time. Then I looked up, across the bar and my eyes locked on the most amazing person I had ever seen. Greg Clark stood at the entrance, all six feet of him, and I couldn't take my eyes off him. It wasn't that he was the most handsome man I had ever seen; however, that did help, but there was "something" about him that made me feel a way I had never felt before and I knew I had to talk to him. Now, I had been to bars before, and I had seen good looking guys, but this one…well he shook me to my core. My girlfriends saw the expression on my face and knew something was captivating me.

"Jenn, what's going on?" said Olivia.

"You see that guy over there?" I said. "I have to talk to him. There is something about him that I am so taken with." They saw the determination in my eyes and knew this was serious business so we strategically planted ourselves in a location where he and his friends were; in between us and the bar.

After passing by several times, he finally noticed me too, and ironically his friends knew mine, which drew our groups together. Olivia made small talk with Greg's friend, Eric, about the music, the night, the town, whatever she could think of, as Greg and I smiled and exchanged flirting glances with each other. After several moments Greg eventually looked at me and threw his hands in the air as if to say, "Are we going to talk or what?"

I motioned for him to come over, he smiled and gave me the universal sign of "Just one minute."

I thought, *Seriously? What is this guy waiting on*? I turned and said the exact same thing to Olivia, and as I turned around he was standing beside me. I immediately asked, "What took you so long, buddy?"

He replied, "Well, I really liked that song, and wanted to finish listening to it." I thought it was hilarious, which instantly broke the ice and our conversation began to flow freely.

"I'm Jenn," I said.

"I'm Ryan…Ryan Sherwood," Greg said. He was about to go on to tell me he was in Las Vegas on business. In fact, he was going to elaborate on how he was in town for a "Homeland Security Conference" as part of his very important job. Unfortunately I beat him to the punch.

"You're in the military, aren't you?" I said.

He looked at me with surprise and nodded.

"Well, don't look so surprised, Ryan. Your haircut gives you away. I'm military too. I'm stationed here, are you?"

Again, he looked at me and nodded his head. We told each other the basics about ourselves; where we were from, what we did, he had a son; I had a cat. We laughed, and danced and had a great time.

At one point, when we were sitting at the bar, he looked up at me and said bashfully, "Jenn, I have a confession to make."

Oh, here it comes, I thought! *This guy is married and instead of one kid he has five! Of course he would! He's too perfect otherwise.*

"Jenn, my name is not really Ryan, its Greg."

"What?"

"Listen! We're in a bar on the strip in Las Vegas," he insisted. "You know as well as I do everyone you meet here is from out of town. What are the chances of meeting someone else who lives here, let alone someone who is also active duty?" I smiled. Little did he know I had done the same thing in the past. I would often tell people my name was "Bernice" or something like that to keep my distance... but not from this guy. I saw the expression of concern on his face that this was the beginning of the end of our incredible encounter.

I figured I would let him sweat it out for a bit. "Well, Greg, how do I know that is your name? Perhaps I should request a formal background check." I was having fun with it, but I could tell he was sincerely sorry.

"No look! Here's my military ID! You see? Gregory Ryan Clark. And if you think about it, technically I wasn't lying completely; see Ryan is my middle name."

I looked at the card and confirmed he was actually who he said he was this time. I also noted the date he entered the service; July 5th, which just so happened to be my birthday. Interesting. Oh, man, I liked him. I decided to let him off the hook, and as the night went on Greg and I started out on what would become our lifelong romance. I will never forget the last song of the night. We danced to "The Dance" by Garth Brooks and I couldn't help but smile about how I almost didn't come out and meet this wonderful man. We exchanged phone numbers and he leaned over and whispered in my ear, "Do you mind if I call you tomorrow and ask you out on a proper first date?"

I smiled and responded, "You better!"

He leaned in again and said simply, "You have my word."

Wowza. My heart was pounding. Such a gentleman! As we said goodnight, I knew there was a special reason why we were brought together that night, even if it was in a bar, on the strip, in Las Vegas of all places.

As promised, he called me the very next day. Our conversation seemed to start right where we left off the night before; it was so easy to talk with him. Ironically I ended up in the hospital the following week due to an unfortunate incident with a cat bite (A piece of advice: don't ever put a scared cat in a bathtub full of water, it doesn't end well). When I told him what happened his playful response was, "Wow, if you didn't want to go out with me, you could have just said so!"

Despite my unlucky circumstances we talked on the phone every day I was admitted and exactly one week after we met, we had our first date. As I watched him walk up to my door, I felt that same feeling that overwhelmed me when I first saw him in the bar. The conversation through the night flowed effortlessly and we laughed and flirted. I got us lost trying to find the restaurant, but we couldn't get enough of each other. When we met, I still thought I was going to pursue the nursing degree, and my package was already submitted. As the evening went on, I couldn't get past the fact I would be leaving in a few short months for school, once I got accepted into the program. I had to be honest with him. I will never forget the conversation: "Greg, listen, I like you a LOT, but, I've got goals, and I am going to finish school and when I get selected for this commissioning program, it means I will be leaving in four months. So... we're going to have to figure this thing out."

He could have responded in so many ways to that, I think most guys would have been like, "Well, see ya!" but he didn't, instead he said, "Wow, that's great that you have such drive. I agree, we are just going to have to find a way to make this thing happen."

I was so lucky to have this man in my life, I thought, as I stood outside my room in Manas. We had such an instant connection when we met, and we have continued to build an incredible friendship. I sat down on the steps and remembered how supportive of me he had always been. I remembered how comforting he was when I was so devastated by the rejection for the nursing program, and how he pushed me to pursue becoming a PA.

As I began completing the prerequisite coursework, Greg and I continued to grow as individuals and as a couple. At one point, I tried to dump him, which is something we laugh about to this day. He was a Security Forces troop and wanted to go to Army Ranger school, which I wanted *nothing* to do with. Anything that was associated with Special Forces was a big fat "no thank you". My infamous words to him, "I am not that girl, Greg. I can't be at home wondering *if*, not *when* you would be coming home. Sorry, I'm not that strong."

I chuckled at the irony of that conversation as I sat in Manas waiting for my flight to go spend six months with the very people I'd wanted no part of so many years ago.

After we broke up, for all of twenty four hours, over that "disagreement," we got past our differences, and fell deeply in love. He became my "Gerg" and I was his "Nej" (our names spelled backwards). His son, Griffen, who was three years old when we met, also became a very special little man in my world. Greg and I moved in together, and he eventually decided to separate from the military. He had come to the conclusion that Ranger school was not for him, and after much thought, he decided it was time to part from active duty.

This was unexpected. When we first met, he was determined the military was going to be his lifelong career. We even had a conversation over sushi one night while I was trying to convince him to go and get his degree. He laughed at me and said, "Why do I need a degree? I love this job, I'm good at it, and this is all I am ever going to do." I was so frustrated with him; I couldn't understand why he wouldn't take advantage of the opportunities that were staring him in the face.

"Gerg, you need to think outside the box. You can't put all of your eggs in your "military basket." What if something happens to you and prevents you from doing what you are now? Then what? All I'm saying is, think beyond your active duty time. Be smart about this!" He was as stubborn as stubborn could be at that time, but he did hear what I was saying. Due to many circumstances with his current squadron and an assignment tasking to Japan he didn't want to take, he made the very difficult decision to walk away from what was once all he ever saw himself doing. How scary it must have been for him.

Two months before my class start date for PA school, he was accepted for a position as a civilian contractor working for KBR as a Security Coordinator in Iraq and Kuwait. I was fearful that once he left, our lives and different paths would pull us apart; but at the same time I trusted that if we were meant to be together then we would be.

To my delight, despite the incredibly demanding time in my life while I was in my first year of school in San Antonio, Greg and I grew even closer, and it became evident he was the one. I had always hoped he would be, but I didn't *know* it until then. He was able to come back to the states from Iraq and Kuwait every three to four months, and chose to spend his time with me in my luxurious 700 sq. ft. apartment with no cable, no food except my staple of chips and salsa, and only my car for transportation. I would leave him early in the morning, get home in the late afternoon and tell him, after not seeing him for months, "Sweetie, you only have two hours of my time, and then I have to study."

Amazingly, he never complained. In fact, he set his watch to ensure I stayed focused on school. He supported me in a way I could never have asked for. I realized that year how truly blessed I was to have such an amazing man.

That December, over my Christmas break, we returned to Las Vegas to visit Griffen. After asking my parents' permission, he proposed in the most romantic way imaginable; in front of the waters at the Bellagio as my favorite song played, Sarah Brightman's "Time to Say Goodbye".

It was a very cold night, and as we stood there waiting for the fountain show to start, I reached into my pocket of my coat and put my gloves on... right before he pulled out the ring. The music started, and I was so happy that it just so happened to be my favorite song. I turned to Greg, smiling with excitement, and he had the ring. He said, "Nej, we started our relationship here, and I felt it only fitting we start the rest of our lives here. Please do me the honor and say you will marry me."

I was filled with joy. I couldn't get those damn gloves off fast enough to put on the ring that meant I would be able to spend the rest of my life with my best friend.

"GERG! Yes!!!!" I screamed. I was so happy in that moment.

When I graduated, we were given a list of assignment options to choose from, and I felt strongly it was Greg's decision to make, so I turned the list over to him. After weighing the options he chose Tyndall AFB to be the place for us to start our next chapter. We arrived in June, and the panhandle of Florida was an unbelievable culture shock from the metropolis of Las Vegas! I felt completely out of place when we first arrived. I cried all the way from the airport to the base. I was used to the big city life, and now I was in the southeastern United States where there were alligators and people shot squirrels and ate them for dinner. It was humid, and gigantic mosquitoes and cockroaches seemed to be everywhere. One day, shortly after we arrived, we took a walk on the base and ended up at the beach which was covered in pure white sand that felt like flour between our toes as we walked. The waters were the most brilliant emerald green I had ever seen, and as we watched our very first sunset we decided we could "deal" with the absolutely breathtaking beauty that surrounded us. We were where we were meant to be. We purchased our very first house as a married couple, and very soon it became our *home*.

Home. I had barely left it and sitting there, going through all of these memories, made me miss it and my life with my Gerg terribly already. I didn't realize how much I had taken for granted, the time I had to spend with loved ones, until that moment.

Day 3
We have a flight

29 April 2008

We finally got scheduled for a flight out of Manas the morning of 30 April at 0600 with a bag drag at 2200 hours which meant we would be checking in our bags. I began to feel nervous about actually getting to Bagram, but excited too; I was ready to get established in what I would be doing. I was able to talk to Greg again. I initially went back to the coffee café but there were so many people I ended up going to the morale phones. I had to wait there too, but it was much more organized and the calls were limited to fifteen minutes. It was so hard to limit the time spent talking to loved ones to just minutes. As I sat there waiting for my turn and thinking about how much the waiting sucked, I looked to my left and my right and I saw a room full of Army soldiers who were on their way home after being deployed for ten to fifteen months waiting to call home too. The difference between them and me was that they weren't complaining one bit. To them, six months was a walk in the park. In that moment I no longer felt sorry for myself; I felt guilty for my selfishness.

At lunch time I caught my first glimpse of the news and saw that two days before, actually the day we arrived in the AOR, there was an assassination attempt on the Afghanistan President, Hamid Karzai, in Kabul, the capital city of the country, about twenty five miles northwest of Bagram. This news was a bit unnerving to me because I knew I would likely be traveling to remote locations throughout the country that could potentially be in the "hot" zone. I had to prepare myself to be exposed to some dangerous situations.

As the day came to an end, we began to get our bags ready to check in at the terminal. After the bag drag was complete, we all agreed to have one last drink at Pete's before we left in the morning. I laid down to rest at about 0130, but didn't sleep at all. I had too many thoughts running through my head about what was to come: *What was in store for me? Would I be strong enough? Would I make the right decisions? How much would I see? Was I prepared to handle the exposure to war and all of its brutal truths?*

CHAPTER 3

Day 4
Saying Hello to Bagram Air Field

30 April 2008

We left Manas in the morning at about 0630 on a C-17. It was my first ride in a military aircraft. As soon as we boarded, we walked into this huge "bay" where there were several palates full of our cargo that we had checked-in at the bag drag the night before. In the center was an area with seats that looked like hand-me-downs from an old civilian aircraft with torn upholstery and heavily-stained fabric. Additional seating was along both sides of the aircraft, facing the center. The ceiling was high and gutted, meaning all of the inner workings of the aircraft were visible. It was exceptionally loud; earplugs were a must-have item. From what I had been told, a C-130 was much louder, so I supposed it could have been worse.

The flight was unique in the fact we had no windows to look out of to get a perspective of where we were in relation to take off or landing. This isolation made touching ground interesting. All I had to rely on was the sounds of the landing gear being released, and sudden change in pressure as we descended. I felt I was at the complete mercy of the beast I was sitting in. How funny, I had experienced the same scenario so many times before, yet it never phased me because I could watch the ground come closer and closer. However, in this situation, not having that visual perception made a tremendous impact to the whole experience. In addition to my newly found perspective on flying, I was filled with various emotions, mainly the feeling of knowing and *not* knowing what was in store for me now that I was there. These feelings sent chills down my spine and my heart into flutters.

As soon as the plane came to a stop and they opened the doors, we all piled out onto the tarmac in two separate lines; Air Force in one line, Army in the other. The flight line was busy with aircraft from all different military forces and countries. It was quite a sight. Some of the aircraft were unlike anything I had ever seen before. The base was surrounded by snowcapped mountains which were quite beautiful. There were buildings all around the flight line that looked very similar to what I experienced on a normal military base in the states. It actually looked like a pretty nice setup and I thought to myself, *This won't be too bad, at least while I am here on Bagram.* We were directed to a very hot, very small tent and began our in-processing with PERSCO. Once we handed over our orders and other required documents, we were released to reacquire our bags and then to report to our duty sections.

While we waited on transportation, we ran into Mike, another friend from our ACST training in the States, who arrived several weeks ahead of us. He was a pilot and knew we would be arriving that day and was happy to greet us. We made small talk and got through the formalities. "We lost a guy yesterday," he told us. "He was a Senior Airman in a convoy just over there," as he pointed to the south mountain range. "He got hit by an IED [Improvised Explosive Device]."

My heart sank. I naively thought, *An Air Force member in a convoy? This just didn't happen, or at least it didn't used to happen. This was what the Army and Marines did - not us.* Even more bizarre, this poor kid was an Aircraft Maintenance troop, so it was unclear to me as to why he was even on a convoy in the first place. I had not felt I was entering into a war zone, until that moment. The land looked normal; the amenities of Manas were tolerable, nothing like the *MASH* episodes I watched on TV as a kid. The food was good, the people were normal....but it became a reality. There were people out there dying. My stomach turned; all of a sudden I wasn't feeling so happy to be there.

Eventually we had someone from Combined Joint Special Operations Task Force Afghanistan (CJSOTF-A) come and take us to where we would be staying. Bagram Airfield (*BAF* I soon learned to call it) was divided up into various camps. Most of the Air Force personnel stayed on Camp Cunningham, but I was attached to Special Forces, so I would be staying in their separate camp. Once we got to our camp I was greeted by a Captain, Bob, a fellow Physician Assistant who had been expecting me.

"Great to meet you Jenn. There is a lot to go over, but for now, I think it's best if you take the rest of today and the next couple of days to get acclimated to the time change and get settled in to your room," he said.

His recommendation was very nice to hear, especially since I had been up for almost twenty-four hours, but I planned on going in the next day to start learning about what I would be doing at the FOBs.

After parting ways with Bob I met up with Becky and Martha. They were two medics I met at my ACST training as well and was told they would likely be working with me once I arrived. I didn't know too much about Martha, but Becky and I hit it off in training and I hoped we would end up working together.

"Lt. Clark!" Becky said. "So glad you made it, I can't wait to fill you in on everything and show you around later, but right now you look exhausted," she said. "I know it's rough getting here."

"Sure is, I'm ready for a nice long shower and sleep," I said.

"Ha! Long shower? We're limited to five minutes tops!" she said, bringing me back to the reality I was deployed.

The rooms were in structures called B-Huts, which were buildings made out of plywood and tin roofs with six to eight separate 9x9 rooms for individuals. I had a twin-size mattress on a wooden bed and a wall locker to store my belongings. The huts did have an AC duct, which worked in the daytime, but due to the lack of insulation and the heat of the climate, the room was still very hot. At night the AC unit didn't shut off, despite the outside temperatures dropping into the 40s. It was not too bad, and certainly could have been worse, but the living conditions still fell under the "rugged living" category compared to what we were used to in the United States. Because I was an officer, I was supposed to get slightly better living conditions in something called a C-Hut, but there were no open rooms. I most likely would not be there long, so I felt there was no need to push the issue, plus I felt sure my B-Hut was luxurious compared to where I would be going.

The dining facility (DFAC) was not bad; actually the food was surprisingly tasty. The food servers were all local Afghan men. As I was walking over to the DFAC, I saw a truck full of them dressed in their tunics and turbans, but for the most part they wore jeans and t-shirts just like us. They were friendly, and some of them were quite handsome. These workers had clean shaven faces and nice neat hair. I thought for sure they would not even acknowledge me; being that I was a woman, but I was wrong. Every time I passed by them, they would say, "Hello, madam," or "How it going, madam?"

The DFAC itself was quite an interesting experience. Keep in mind that on a Special Forces camp there were typically little-to-no females. Becky and I walked into the room and I instantly felt all eyes on us and could see the whispering and the winks and I felt completely singled out and an instant "object". I knew it would be like this when I left, but couldn't really prepare for it until I actually got there. The majority of the men in the Special Forces camp were in the same unit back at Fort Bragg, which meant they worked together in the States and deployed together every six to eight months as a big team. The current group would be starting to filter out the next day and the new group would begin to come in.

"The Group here keeps saying the new guys are arrogant and cocky," Becky said.

"Great! Just what we need," I replied. "For an SF guy to say that, they must be pretty bad."

CHAPTER 4

Day 5
The Flashing Light

1 May 2008

I finished getting my B-Hut squared away the next morning and then decided it was time to go to the gym for a workout. Prior to this deployment I had really let myself slip in the physical fitness department, mainly due to stress, time, and any other excuse I could find. I had been "lazy" since I started PA school and it had become a bad habit since. I hated sitting in my exam room with my patients who had chronic medical conditions such as diabetes, hypertension, and high cholesterol and preaching the latest American Heart Association guidelines on physical activity, yet not following the same practices myself. I vowed before I left to make the lifestyle change while I was deployed, and continue the practice back home. So far the renewed activity had been a welcomed change. I loved getting back into my routine at the gym. I would leave feeling so good about my workout and what I had accomplished….that was until this day.

I was midway through my run on the treadmill and in my "zone" when Tony arrived. "How long has that red light been going off?" he asked me.

"What light?" I asked. He pointed to a flashing red light on the north wall of the gym. "Oh, that light. I have no idea," I said. "Why?"

"That light is an alert that's used to let us know that there is some sort of active 'contact' with our SF guys outside the wire," he explained.

"When you say *contact*, what do you mean exactly?" I asked.

"Anything like an IED, sniper fire, a fire fight, maybe the firebase getting attacked, or any other form of enemy attack or encounter," he explained.

I had no idea such a system of alert was in place. Throughout the remainder of my workout I couldn't keep my eyes off of that light, praying it would stop flashing, but it didn't. I looked around the gym in amazement at the lack of response to this "beacon of danger" from the Special Forces guys working out around me. Why weren't they terrified and running from the building to assist their friends? Why were they laughing and joking with each other and carrying on as if nothing was happening?

Then it hit me. This was a form of normalcy for them. This was what they did every day. This was a routine day in the life of Army Special Forces troops, a day they spent years training for.

My new awareness of the light was haunting. I didn't ever want to see it flash again. Unfortunately, the reality was I *would* see it again; many times over, and there was nothing I could do to change it. The one thing I could do was to continue to let it affect me the way it had that day. I never wanted to react any other way.

CHAPTER 5

Day 6
Medic Warriors

2 May 2008

In the morning I went to Sick Call with Becky and Martha. The Sick Call was a one-hour clinic in the morning and again in the afternoon, which was typically technician run, yet I was bored and figured what the heck? While I was there, I got to talk more with the PA, Bob, and the leadership of the group about some things to expect out there.

"The most common types of medical conditions you can expect are things like acid reflux, arthritis, dehydration, asthma, malnutrition, and a lot of dermatology and orthopedic conditions. You are going to see plenty of traumas, so be prepared," Bob explained.

"What kind of living conditions can we expect?" Becky chimed in.

"You will likely be in a fixed facility. Each firebase is different, but most are somewhat better than the B-huts we have here," he said. "Bathrooms are hit or miss. So is the food. Most firebases try to have some kind of workout area, but usually it's not much."

"What about safety?" I asked, knowing the answer was not going to be what either Becky or I wanted to hear.

"Again, it depends on where you go. You will likely travel to multiple places, at least initially. I know they are thinking of sending you to a couple of different locations in the Uruzgan Province, which is currently a violent area, so you should anticipate contact," Bob explained. There was that word again. He continued, "You need to prepare for that to happen and you may need to participate in combat if the firebase is attacked."

What!!? Becky and I shared the same disbelief. Our expressions clearly asked "Who? *Me?*" When I joined the Air Force and went through my training as a medic, I was told about the Geneva Conventions and that by being a medic I was considered a "noncombatant," which meant I was not allowed to engage in combat. I was told I could carry a weapon, but not fire it unless I was protecting my patients. Based on my career field I had infrequent training on the firing range; usually qualifying once every twenty-four months. Qualifying meant I had to hit the target on the range a certain amount of times within the standards set by the Air Force; I did this before I left Tyndall. In addition, I completed the two week course in ACST. The course was designed to give the students an understanding of what to expect in a combat situation; depending on the deployment, sometimes it was three months long instead of just fourteen days. Even during that training, I thought, *I will do this exercise, but it doesn't apply to me; I won't be in these situations.* I had developed a false sense of security behind my noncombatant title.

Bob could see our concern. "Don't worry," he said reassuringly, "You likely wouldn't be actively engaging in a fire fight per say, but helping to load mortar rounds and ammunition would certainly be something you would potentially be asked to do."

Becky and I looked at each other knowing we were both feeling the same unease.

Bob chuckled as he continued, "You guys will get to fire some weapons out there you may have never even heard of. All you have to do is show an active interest and the guys would be more than happy to let you practice out at the range."

I couldn't even begin to explain the thoughts going through my head. I knew I was a part of the military, and use of force was something that we did, but I couldn't imagine myself in a situation where I would have to engage. As I pondered this thought, I realized the majority of active duty military members, combatant or noncombatant, probably had experienced a very similar mindset. Yes, we signed the dotted line, but did you really mean we had to go to war?

I was also introduced to the radio room. It was located in the back of the Med Shed and the medics, which now included both Becky and Martha, were trained to monitor the radios and document all medical evacuations, forwarding all necessary information to the people who required it. I learned this could be very stressful. When there was an altercation going on with our Special Forces units a red light would flash (just like the one I saw at the gym) and the door would close, which meant if you weren't necessary for the radios then you were instructed to leave the room.

More flashing red lights to serve as a reminder of what was happening out there.

We were asked about the weapons we were issued back at our home stations. As an officer, I was given only an M9 (9mm pistol) and the medics were given M16 rifles.

They laughed and told us not to worry; they would give us what we needed to go out in the field. I got issued an M4, which is a rifle, the exact same makeup as an M16, but with a shorter barrel and a collapsible stock. We were then sent out to the range to "zero our weapon." which consisted of firing at a specific target until the sights were adjusted to the person firing the weapon.

"I can take you," one of the non-medical guys offered, "I have to go out there anyway."

Becky and I smiled at each other. "I bet you do," Becky whispered jokingly in my ear. I laughed.

"Ok, ladies, let's step over here and let's get those M4s zeroed," our escort said as he strutted by.

"Sure thing Rambo," I whispered to Becky. We couldn't help but giggle.

I zeroed my weapon relatively quickly and wanted to practice firing my M9. Initially I had a lot of trouble with my aim. This was frustrating for me because I had a 9mm back home and was used to firing. Another soldier saw I was frustrated and offered to help. His intentions seemed genuine, so I agreed. He stood and assessed what I was doing for several minutes and then he spoke.

"Ma'am, you're anticipating pulling the trigger, and it's causing you to dip the barrel." He was right. I had done that in the past. He reminded me of breathing techniques and how to *squeeze* the trigger and my shot was instantly fixed. I fired my entire magazine and had a nice close grouping right on target, which made me smile.

"Where did that come from?" he asked. "I think you are a better shot than I am. Nice work."

I was actually enjoying being out there firing, it reminded me of several times Greg and I spent together on the range back home, and of the times I fired my dad's rifles and pistols as a kid. The fears from the conversation with Bob earlier, which had been forefront on my mind when we started the day, left my thoughts; I was having fun.

While we were out there, we met some Australian SF guys who had an AK-47. I'd heard about the weapon in books, on the news, and of course in training, but had never seen one.

"Would you like to take a shot with it?" they asked.

"Yes!" was my response. I never in a million years thought I would fire one of those, and I had to admit, it was pretty cool.

The range was an experience in and of itself, but the most memorable experience for me was not firing an AK-47, but the trip out to the range. It was quite a distance from the camp we were staying on, so we had to drive the perimeter of the base to get there. Along the perimeter we were able to see outside the wire for the first time; along the roads and in the fields the ground was covered with old Russian machinery in ruins from the Soviet War. Our driver told us that some of the FOBs actually had old MIGs and tanks just sitting on the base that never got removed. How crazy. Such a horrible piece of history was staring me in the face.

The living conditions of the people were something right out of Native American history. Their "buildings" looked more like ruins made of bricks created out of mud with no doors, and no floors, no bathroom or any form of air conditioning or heating unit. It reminded me very much of Indian Pueblos. I found it absolutely fascinating and tragic at the same time. How could we, as Americans, take everything we had so much for granted? It made me feel ashamed of the wasteful habits I had formed in America. As we drove past we saw children running as fast as they could along the fence line waving and shouting "Chocolate! Chocolate!" in Pashtu, the native language of that region of Afghanistan. They seemed so small and innocent and so unfairly subjected to the poverty they lived in; seeing how they reacted to us warmed my heart. The children continued to wave as we lost sight of them.

I began to feel everything was going to be ok. I thought to myself, *I may have to be a part of this war in ways I didn't anticipate. I may have to put on the "warrior" hat if it comes down to it with the Taliban, but I am always a medic at heart and knowing what I am about to do for these people makes sense.* I was in a position that was unique. I would have an opportunity to reach out to the women and children of these poverty-stricken people and make a difference that very few people get the opportunity to make. And that was why I was there.

CHAPTER **6**

Day 7
How Bazaar

3 May 2008

It was my first experience with the bazaar – in the Middle East this is a large, open market place where the people barter their goods. Everything from dishes made of jade and rugs made of Afghan wool, to hand-carved wooden items, gems, and silk scarves were sold. Often times it was the place where the people would go to receive medical care from the "bazaar doctor." Once a week Bagram opened its gates and hosted a secured bazaar at various locations on base allowing the locals to set up shop and sell their goods to Coalition Forces. The salesmen had any and everything to offer, the problem was they didn't like to take "No" for an answer!

"Madam! Please! Come and see! You like rug for you? Wait! Perhaps you like pashmina scarf? Here try on...No wait. Look at these blankets. You like necklace? Here. I give good deal," they would say, wanting to show us *everything* they had for sale in hopes we would change our minds and purchase something. It felt uncomfortable.

"No, thank you. No, sir, no thank you!" I keep saying, feeling somewhat obligated to barter a deal. I did leave with a small purchase I went into the day knowing I would make. I acquired a large blanket with 2 pillowcases for a very reasonable price, at least that is what the salesman said. I saw a lot of things I would consider purchasing in the future, but I thought I would do my research first and figure out what exactly a *good deal* really was.

It was also a Colonel's birthday so after the bazaar we had a celebration with a barbeque and some members of the Air Force band came out to perform. They were really good and the performance turned out to be quite entertaining. It felt like a little piece of home, as we listened to classic American songs and sang along. What a fun job that must be, doing nothing but improving the morale of the troops that are in often unpleasant situations. I'd met several band members in training and they all seemed to love what they did. I was amazed at the level of talent they possessed; some had even written and recorded songs with famous artists in Nashville. What an amazing and important impact their services had on our troops.

CHAPTER 7

Day 14
Salute to a Fallen Comrade

10 May 2008

I hadn't written on days 8-13 because they all seemed to run together and were exactly identical to each other. Everything was in a standstill until the new leadership arrived, so I was basically there with no real role. The days started with me waking up at 0700 and getting dressed. Around the same time Greg was usually online so we would chat as I got ready. At 0800 I went to breakfast and got my standard egg white omelet with ham and cheese and a bowl of oatmeal. Already the food was beginning to taste the same and I often found myself eating very little at lunch and dinner, so I made every effort to go to breakfast since it was the only meal I enjoyed. After I finished breakfast I went to Sick Call at 0900. As I mentioned before, this had been a medic run clinic, but since the old unit was leaving and the new one was coming in, they needed room to medically out-process people; therefore, an all-day Sick Call had become necessary for a short period of time. During this time a provider needed to be present and since the Army providers were tied up with the out-processing I was it. My mornings consisted of several hours of reading up on medical literature and seeing one or two patients at a time, which was a far cry from what my clinic was like back home. Most of the patients were not even "patients." They were people needing allergy medicine or sunscreen or something else very minor. Every once in a while I would do something worthwhile. One day I did a toenail removal and it was the most exciting part of my day.

At noon I ate lunch and popped in and out of the clinic in the afternoons until 1900, making myself available until it closed if they needed me. At 1930 I headed to the gym and I was there for about an hour and a half; then I came home, showered, and went to bed. The next day it started all over again. I was accepting this schedule, as mundane as it was, as my new reality. I was becoming more comfortable, more relaxed and feeling somewhat "safe" in my environment.

At approximately 0500 a very loud and annoying sound woke me from my not-so-sound sleep. It was an overhead announcement that was loud enough to be heard base wide: "ATTENTION! ATTENTION! A FALLEN COMRADE CEREMONY WILL BE HELD AT 0550, ALL AVAILABLE PERSONNEL ARE TO FALL OUT. PT GEAR AND PHOTOGRAPHY ARE PROHIBITED."

I lay in bed still groggy and trying to figure out what had just been said. It was so early. I had slept horribly the night before and was craving more rest. I tried to convince myself that I was "*un*available" and it was ok to fall back asleep; after all, who would even notice if I wasn't there? I found the more I tried to convince myself it was okay to sleep, the more awake I became and the reality of the situation emerged from the foggy haze of my sleep deprivation. For God's sake, Jenn. Someone *died*.

I hurried out of bed and threw on my uniform and hat. I had to stop and pick up my 9mm, because outside of our camp we were required to be in uniform and have a weapon on us at all times. After I got my firearm I rushed out the gate of the camp to the main road of Bagram. Once I stepped out of the gate, what I saw was breathtaking. The street was lined on both sides with hundreds of military members from all branches of service, all standing at parade rest. Despite the fact there were hundreds of people in one place, it was absolutely silent. Not a word was spoken by anyone, not even the youngest

Private. It was the most somber feeling.

As I stood there, my mind drifted. I wondered who it was that gave his or her life and under what circumstances. I wondered if there was a spouse and children who would be left behind, and if the family had already been notified.

After several minutes we saw a convoy that consisted of a police SUV with the lights flashing that carried a passenger hanging out the window with a video camera filming the scene. Following the police vehicle were two High Mobility Multi-Wheeled Vehicles (HMMWVs); the second HMMWV carried the casket of our fallen comrade, draped with the American flag. As they approached, we all snapped to attention, saluted, and held the salute long after they passed. And that was it. The video footage taken would be given to the loved ones of the fallen soldier. It was the most beautiful, horrible moment I had experienced. As I walked back to my B-hut, I vowed right then and there that I would be present for every future ceremony that I could possibly be there for. It was the absolute least I could do.

CHAPTER 8

Day 19
One Year Later

18 May 2008

Exactly one year ago on this day I was commissioned as First Lieutenant as I graduated from PA school with my Master's degree. Who would have thought I would be spending the anniversary of such a monumental day in my life over 7,000 miles away from home? It could not have been more fitting that on this anniversary I attended an officer professional development briefing with a Brigadier General as our guest speaker. During his prepared speech he talked about what we, as officers, needed in order to be successful in leading our troops.

"The key traits of successful leaders are simple; they consist of courage, caring, competence, and a valid interpretation of the truth. Without any of these things you will fail your troops," he said. "Equally important is loyalty and sense of duty. These things are imperative for any effective officer."

His speech was typical of what I expected; motivational yet not anything I hadn't heard before. "Sir," a Lt. Col asked, "can you please elaborate on what to say to all the young officers who are getting out of the service so quickly into their careers. How can we convince them to stay?" The General's response was undoubtedly unexpected and as I listened to his words I felt he was speaking directly to my heart.

"Well, this might surprise some of you, but I am not the type of person to try to keep people in the service any longer than they want to be in; I'm just grateful they served their country at all." The tone of the room shifted. He had everyone's full and undivided attention. He continued, "I completely understand why young officers are getting out. Let's face it; we're in the military in a time of war, a war that is not ending any time soon. This is a truth that is extremely difficult to deal with. Since 9/11 I have deployed a total of four times, each tour lasting fifteen months. I can't even begin to count the number of birthdays, anniversaries, holidays, and special occasions I have missed because of this job."

I couldn't even imagine having to sacrifice that much of myself.

He continued, "As if those sacrifices weren't enough, let's talk about what realities we all face while we're here. In my previous command I lost twenty-nine soldiers and in my current command I have already lost eleven. People's *lives* are gone forever. This job has no material rewards, and the compensation we do receive is far less than the sacrifice we are asked to make every day." His words pierced the silence in the room. As painful as it was to hear, we all knew he was right.

"The only thing we can really take from our service is knowing we are a part of something much bigger than ourselves. In just 2001, they were taking women in this country to the sports arena and blowing their heads off because they showed their ankles, or slitting men's throats because they allowed their daughters to go to school. In that short time ago, less than 10% of Afghan people had access to healthcare, and now, seven years later, over 80% do. Little girls were once completely banned from school, now we are building schools especially for these same girls. Women are slowly gaining back the respect they once had before the Taliban," he said.

As I listened to him talk about the women and little girls, my eyes filled with tears. I couldn't imagine having to live in such fear and oppression.

"But we all know that this positive impact doesn't come without a cost," he went on. "Our soldiers are dying. Let me tell you the story of two young Lieutenants I once commanded. They were very motivated individuals who often came to me for advice on their careers, and eventually I convinced them that becoming Special Forces was a great opportunity. Now both of those men are dead. They were killed in action. And don't any of you think that a day goes by I don't think about how I was responsible for their deaths."

"Sir, can you tell us how you balance your life?" another person from the audience asked. "Specifically your work and sense of duty with your family, and what advice could you give to us on how we can do so as well?"

The General looked at him and laughed. "Balance?" he asked. "What balance? You ask my wife and children about the balance and you will see who has gotten the short end of the deal for twenty-five years. In my job, as in so many of ours, there is no balance," he said. "There is just an understanding the military comes first. This is a huge thing to ask of people and it is an even bigger sacrifice for the family members to make year after year."

I found so much of my own thoughts to be completely in sync with his. I'd always promised myself as long as I got out of the military what I had put in to it, then I would stay, and when that changed it would be time for me to explore other options. Looking back on my career I could see that promise held true and I had been fortunate to get what I had out of my military experience. Hell! I'd just finished my Bachelor's and Master's degrees and got paid to do it! I had known deep down I needed to deploy and serve my country to repay everything I had gotten from the Air Force; and this deployment was giving me the opportunity to reach out and make a real difference to a population of people, specifically the women and little girls, that had no previous healthcare. But this opportunity did not come without cost. Being away from family for six months was cost enough, but it was dangerous as well. Some of the potential places they were asking me to go to were extremely active with Taliban and there was a very real possibility I could encounter their actions firsthand.

I knew once this experience was over, I would never want to come back. That voice deep inside my gut was telling me on this date, in the year 2011, it would be time for me to turn in my combat boots and begin a new life. My priorities were different now. They constantly ingrained in us we had to put the mission first, before anything, and some people are able to do that for twenty years and beyond. I couldn't anymore. My family was much too important to me. I was proud to be able to say I had spent time in Afghanistan and made my contribution, but life was too short, and I knew I couldn't spend much more of mine making these sacrifices.

This day was the most fitting anniversary of my commissioning. I received a message from a General that made all of the thoughts I had been feeling for such a long time okay for me to feel.

CHAPTER 9

Day 28
Final Destination Revealed

25 May 2008

The Special Forces Groups finally made the switch and we met the majority of the people who would be in charge of the Med Shed. They all seemed nice, not at all the "cocky" guys we had been told to expect. The man in charge was a Family Practice Physician we all learned to call "Doc". Once the new group was settled in, we got official word of where we were going. After one month of waiting.... we were assigned to Firebase Anaconda. It was the more violent of the two firebases in the Uruzgan Province. The location we had suspected was now certain. It was a very dangerous area, but we were informed the clinic had already been well established and were reassured we would be well taken care of.

I was also informed Becky would be accompanying me. I had grown to like her very much and respected her eagerness to learn and grow as a medic. My initial impression of her back in our ACST training, prior to the deployment, was validated. I knew we would work well together and had pushed to get her assigned to go with me. We still had no definite date of departure, but it tentatively would be in the next seven to ten days.

As the location of our destination was revealed, word spread throughout the camp, and Becky and I faced shocked faces and reactions of disbelief. "They are sending YOU to *THAT* place? *Are you kidding?*"

The more we heard that reaction, the more uneasy we became. We were asked to conduct an interview for Public Relations requested by the Group Commander to discuss the Female Treatment Team (FTT) and our role in it. The interview apparently was for a press release to disclose the valuable asset the FTT was to both the Afghanistan people and our forces in their country. The PR representative said she would likely follow the press release with a full article about us in the future and asked for our contact information to follow up. She asked us questions on what we were feeling, knowing we would be the only females out there in such a forward location, and what it meant to us personally to know we were going to be a part of something so much bigger than ourselves.

As I answered her questions, it hit me just how big this was. Yes, it was potentially very dangerous but it was an experience of a lifetime. If, God forbid, something did happen to me out there, I felt I could take comfort in knowing I was making a difference in the most direct way imaginable.

After the interview we finished talking with our leadership and took in all the stories of previous experiences and advice they had to offer. "An important thing for you both to remember is to avoid wearing perfume all together when you are out there," said Don, a new male PA.

"Why?" I asked. "Is it due to the bugs?"

"No, it will likely be yet another distraction to the team guys, and the last thing you want to do is bother them," he explained. I never would have thought of that as a distraction, but it seemed to make sense. "Now that we know you guys are going to one of the most violent firebases in Afghanistan, it is vital that you get as much training on the equipment out there as you can. You need to become so familiar with the various buttons and switches in the vehicles that you could operate them blindfolded if need be."

"Can you elaborate?" Becky asked.

"Think of it this way, most attacks will occur at night. You need to be prepared to defend yourselves."

Becky and I listened, exchanging "Oh my God" looks, knowing we would be all each other had for the next five months. The more we talked to Don, the more we realized how ill-prepared we were. As we discussed the gear we would need for what we would be doing, Don shook his head in frustration. "You guys don't have the equipment I think you need to go out there. I want to get you issued what you don't have and replace some of the items you do have."

"What do you think we need to replace?"

"Your body armor, cold weather gear, individual first aid kits (IFAKs) to start. You were sent here with standard issue items, but this is not a standard place you are going. You need to be equipped with the same equipment as the guys you're going out with."

"Thanks Don. I appreciate you making sure we are ready," I said.

It was in the remaining days we were at BAF we got all of our new and improved gear squared away, continued our medical training with a stronger emphasis on trauma, and packed up our belongings. Don continued to ensure we had everything we needed to go out, which was interesting because we later found out he had grown to "hate" all females that were attached to their teams because they all seemed to be "easy" and a huge distraction for the team guys. We thankfully managed to change his perception, which was a godsend, as we desperately needed his help to prepare for what was ahead of us.

I wished I could find the exact words to describe what I was feeling as I prepared mentally and physically for my upcoming adventure...but I couldn't because there weren't any.

CHAPTER 10

Days 32 and 33
One of Our Own

30 May and 1 June 2008
   30 May 2008
   I knew in the back of my mind it was likely to happen, but I prayed it wouldn't. Doc came into the Med Shed with a look of shock and disbelief that morning.
   "Are you ok?" I asked him. However, I knew full well he was far from ok.
   "No, I'm not Jennifer. We lost one of our own from our unit yesterday," he said. Up until then, all of the Fallen Comrade ceremonies had been for someone outside of the Special Forces personnel; making them distant enough for me to dissociate, but this one was much different. He had been on a mission and was killed in action due to a secondary blast from an IED. Because he was in our unit, our participation in the Fallen Comrade ceremony was much more intimate. Instead of lining the sides of the main street of the base, we formed up on the flight line to be present when the remains entered the aircraft that would fly him home.
   The day leading up to the ceremony was melancholy. I sensed such pain in the faces and eyes of the soldiers I worked with, especially Doc. His grandfather had been a prisoner of war, and he took

all of what we were doing out there very much to heart. He was quiet the whole day; preoccupied with ensuring the fallen soldier's team members, who were also injured in the mission, were taken care of to the best of everyone's capabilities. He wanted someone greeting them at the hospital, at the flight line when they were arriving, and when they were leaving.

The ceremony was held at 0001 (12:01am) due to the flight schedule of the aircraft. As we lined up waiting, we watched the color guard practice over and over again to make sure they had their job down flawlessly. I watched them stand at parade rest and a senior NCO walked behind them and checked their pant legs were properly bloused and their hands behind their backs were all at the same level and looked exactly the same. He brushed off their uniforms and made sure their hats were on straight. Every small detail was important.

A cordon was formed of the soldiers who worked closely with the deceased that led from the flight line to the rear of the C-130 that would be flying him home. I looked at the plane and noticed the flight crew sweeping the floor and straightening the bay and lastly hanging an American flag facing outside. The pallbearers consisted of the members on his team who were not injured. They wore their green berets and white gloves and their duty uniforms. As I watched them standing there waiting on their friend I noticed not a word was spoken between them. They had blank stares on their faces, trying not to show any emotion at such a hurtful time. The band members lined up to the right of the cordon and prepared their instruments while a soldier with a bagpipe stood 100 meters down the flight line, alone at parade rest waiting for the vehicles.

As the vehicles turned onto the flight line the soldier with the bagpipe snapped to position and began playing "Amazing Grace". As we stood there listening, I became overwhelmed with emotion for someone I had never met. Tears welled up in my eyes as the vehicle slowly passed in front of me. I was honored to be present for the heartfelt ceremony sending him home. The HMMWV that carried his casket drove past us and parked just to the side of the pallbearers. They stood at attention until it reached a complete stop and ceremoniously took their friend from the bed of the vehicle and slowly marched up through the cordon to the plane. As they did the band began to play with the bagpipes. Once they lowered the casket, they stepped off the plane and the door slowly closed. As we walked back to our camp I was speechless with emotion. It was a beautiful tribute, yet I never wanted to see another one again.

1 June 2008

At 0900 the memorial service was given for our fallen friend. We listened to the invocation and opening remarks by the presiding two-star General. Then each of his team members spoke about memories of their good friend. They talked about his personality, his work ethic, and his wife and two sons he left behind. It was heartbreaking to listen to these men, who are the toughest of the tough, men who were fearless to face any battle, break down into tears in front of hundreds of people.

I couldn't imagine the loss they must have felt. These guys worked together on these teams for years and years and became a family. They saw and did things no one outside of their own team could truly understand. When all the speeches were finished, we prayed again and then a roll call commenced. It was started by the senior ranking officer of the battalion who called the names of the team members. Each soldier replied with a "Here Sir!" until he reached the name of the deceased. He called his name and waited; he called again and waited, and then again one last time.

After the final failure of response, the ceremony closed with a 21 gun salute. The music began to play and a line formed, filled with people who wished to pay their respects, which was headed by the men on his team. The line led to the front of the flagpoles which had his boots, weapon, helmet, dog tags, and several pictures of him honorably displayed.

Before I got in line, I stood and watched the team say one last goodbye. They marched up in pairs and stopped six feet in front of his belongings, saluted, and proceeded forward. When they arrived in front of his things, they took a knee and had a moment of silence. One of the guys reached forward and grabbed his friend's dog tags and instantly began to sob. He stayed on his knee for several minutes, struggling with the knowledge that when he let go of the dog tags he would be letting go of his friend as well. He finally managed to stand, and they backed up and stopped again at six feet away and saluted one last time. Once the entire team had completed this, they stood to the side and allowed everyone else to say goodbye.

I stood at the end of line, feeling so much emotion for everyone involved. I felt almost out of place; I had no concept whatsoever of what these guys did or the true sacrifices they made with their frequent deployments and losses of friends. Regardless, I absolutely wanted to pay my respects and patiently waited while the line slowly moved forward. Before I knew it I was standing six feet away, saluting, moving forward and taking a knee.

As I looked at his face I began to cry for this man who was a complete stranger to me. He'd made the ultimate sacrifice, and finally seeing the face behind the name moved me beyond words. As I stood, backed up and saluted one last time, I looked at his team standing off to the side. I felt compelled to go to them. I shook their hands one by one. There was so much I wanted to say, but no words would come. Looking into their eyes I realized that no words were necessary. It was an unspoken moment between service members that needed no explanation. After shaking the last hand, I sighed deeply, wiped away my tears and went back to work. We all did.

CHAPTER 11

Day 37
Here We Go

5 June 2008

We finally left for our firebase after nearly a month and a half of waiting. Even though my deployment was 1/6 of the way over, it felt like it was the first day. My nerves were all over the place as I anticipated the future. We had been waiting and waiting and preparing as best as we could and the moment had finally arrived. As Becky and I packed we tried to comfort each other as best we could; knowing we were both thinking of the same things.

"Are we going to be okay out there? I mean, surely they're prepared for us being there, right?" Becky asked.

"I sure hope so. What do you think our husbands would say if they knew where we were going?" I responded.

"I think they would say: Are you *serious*? You are sending our wives *where?*" she laughed.

"I know. I honestly think Greg would lose his mind if he knew what I was about to do."

"Mike would be on the phone with his congressman!" she joked. "Seriously, Jenn- I mean Lt. Clark," she stumbled.

"Becky, in all honesty, we're beyond formalities now. Knowing where we are going, you have absolute permission to call me Jenn."

"Ok, but I still respect your rank, and the fact you're an officer. Seriously, *Jenn*, I am so thankful it's you I am going out there with. I can't think of any other provider I would be more comfortable working with."

"Thank you," I said through my tears. "I honestly feel the same way about you. We're going to be ok; in fact, we are going to be *great*. We will take so much away from this, and working together as a team is going to be a great experience for us."

"You are so right," she said.

I gave her a big hug. We both held on as tightly as we could, knowing our bond was already stronger than either of us could have anticipated. As we embraced, I couldn't help but question what I'd just said. I meant everything, I just hoped I wasn't lying; that it *would* be a great experience for us both, but I knew only time would tell.

I packed as many of my belongings as I could into a 2x3 foot locker, my duffle bag, and a backpack. I also had to carry both my M9 and M4 with my body armor. All of the gear and belongings made up quite a load for me to tackle. Luckily, we had some friends see us off at the terminal who helped carry our things. Prior to our departure we had to go by the personnel office and fill out some "paperwork".

When we arrived, we were given a stack of documents containing several questions I never wanted to answer. *If killed in the field, who would you like to escort your body home? What type of ceremony do you request at your funeral? What would you like to be done with your remains? Do you have any wishes for your personal belongs?*

As I filled out the paperwork I felt sick. There was a real possibility I could *die*. After I completed what seemed like a never-ending list of unimaginable questions, we were escorted to the next hut over. We needed to take a picture in front of the flag in case there was a need for a memorial service. As I stood in front of the flag, I wondered: *Do I smile? Should I look serious? How would I want people to remember me?* I decided to smile and before I knew it the Army Private snapped the photo.

"That's it?" I asked.

"Yes ma'am, that's it," he said.

I prayed it was a good shot and my eyes weren't closed or I had a goofy look on my face. I certainly hoped, now of all times, that the young Private caught my "good side."

We left on a C-130, yet another aircraft to add to my ever-growing list of military aircraft I had flown on. As I walked onto the plane, a fellow Air Force member, whom I soon discovered was the crew chief, pointed at me and said, "You! Come with me! I have a special seat for you." I looked around to verify he was indeed talking to me, and when I saw no one else standing around me, I followed his instruction and followed him to the front of the plane. He led me to a ladder and helped me up into the flight deck.

"Are you kidding?" I asked. "I really get to sit up here?"

He nodded and of course immediately I asked him if Becky and Megan (an Army Preventative Medicine technician traveling with us) could come and sit up front too. He went back and got them and we all three sat there smiling ear to ear about this cool experience. It was obvious we were chosen because we were female, but heck! Who cared? It was my first ride on a C-130, and what better seats then the flight deck?

The pilots were friendly, and happy to explain everything to us. I found it fascinating to see how they operated such a huge machine. They were flying us down to Kandahar Air Field (KAF) where we would be for a couple of days and then we would fly out again to our firebase. The flight was just over an hour which passed very quickly.

We were met by some of the guys we had known from Bagram that left before us, as well as some of the Med Shed personnel at KAF. They helped us with our baggage and got us situated in our rooms. Once we dropped everything off we went to the Med Shed where we met our new "Doc" who was responsible for RC-South region of Afghanistan, who also became known to me as the "Bearer of Bad News". He informed us there was a slight change in plans and now Becky would be going on to our firebase without me temporarily, and I would be staying back to participate in a "MedCap" - a group of medical providers who went to a location within a village and provided medical treatment and dispensed humanitarian aid supplies to masses of people. MedCaps were created both to reach out to the people and their healthcare needs and to gather intelligence. Despite how wonderful the cause was, I was a little uncomfortable about participating in this adventure. The region we were in was very active with conflict involving the Taliban, and I had become quite accustomed to being safe "behind the wire". I was hoping I wouldn't have to go out in any convoys into unsecured areas, but it became evident that was not the case. I was also upset about being separated from Becky. We had become so used to having each other as a crutch to deal with the situation we were in, but now I would be on my own for several weeks in what could be the scariest part of the deployment yet.

"Jenn, how can they separate us?" Becky asked that night in our new B-hut. "What are we going to do without each other?"

I didn't have an answer, I had the same questions. All I could say was, "Don't worry, Becks; we'll be back together before we know it." We were both scared for very different reasons that night. She would be moving on to the firebase and into the unknown alone, while I had to go on a completely unexpected mission without her. We hugged tightly and spent the remainder of the night talking, finding comfort for one last night with the only friend either one of us really had for the remainder of our deployment.

After I left Becky, and lay down to sleep, I couldn't help but notice the faint sound of gunfire in the background. It was just people firing at the range, but it confirmed my fears that I had definitely entered the combat zone, in more ways than one.

CHAPTER **12**

Day 44
The "No Limit" Soldier Has Limits

12 June 2008

Unlike Bagram, Kandahar Airfield was run by the Canadians, not the United States. Overall it was a nice installation. It had a "boardwalk" with amenities like Subway and Burger King and the Starbucks Coffee of Canada called Tim Horton's. I must admit, the coffee was very tasty. The airfield was nationally divided; the Canadian, British, Dutch, and Americans all had their respective compounds. The British compound was unbelievable; they had a coffee shop that was nicer than some in the United States! It had white leather chairs, flat-screen televisions and some sort of fabulous contraption that produced fresh squeezed orange juice from whole oranges with the touch of a button.

Becky left for the firebase on the 7th which left me to prepare for the MedCap. I spent five days working hours and hours to prepare the supplies, doing things like loading up huge Pelican cases (which were similar to large footlockers) full of medications and making individual bags of the most commonly used medications like anti-inflammatories, multivitamins, and antacids. It was a lot of busy work, but it was all going to a good cause and I had nothing better to do. I eventually ended up with four Pelican cases and a large tri-fold box filled with

THE "NO LIMIT" SOLDIER HAS LIMITS

supplies that would be palletized and loaded in to the aircraft when we left.

The day I was scheduled to leave for the MedCap site was also the day I realized this "No Limit" soldier did, in fact, have limits. In all honesty, I had come to find a pleasing comfort in the sheltered life I had lived for the past eight years. Once Becky left, I became the only Air Force member surrounded by not just Army, but Special Forces Army with all of their field experiences to boot.

As I listened to their stories, I quite frankly wanted to crawl into my Air Force uniform and disappear. I realized just how different we were and how different our training had been. They were fully prepared for battle on the ground, and all that came with it, whereas I was not in the least. I was reminded again of my previous false sense of security in being medical personnel. As Vance, a Special Forces medic, Megan and I waited for our helicopter; they decided to exchange combat stories with each other. Vance brought up the Chinook helicopter crash he responded to on his last deployment that was shot down with no survivors. This was my first helicopter experience, and ironically, we happened to be flying on a Chinook. He and Megan continued their talk about responding to enemy fire and killing bad guys; I looked down at my hands and realized my fists were clenched tightly around the bag I was holding. I set the bag down and walked away from the conversation, feeling I needed air; my fear was beginning to suffocate me.

When the bird arrived Vance nudged me, "Hey, don't forget to put on your gloves," as he pointed to my flak vest where they were clipped.

"Why?" I asked.

"Protection for your hands in case the Chinook gets shot up and catches fire," he answered. My hands began to shake as I reached for the gloves and unclipped them from my vest. I tried to hide them and quickly donned the gloves and put my shaking hands to my sides. "Also, make sure you have a magazine in your M4 and M9 locked and loaded just in case," he continued.

"Got it, thanks," I answered and prepared my weapons.

Once Vance, Megan, the other passengers, me, and my bag of nerves, got on the Chinook and seat-belted in I pretended none of the previous conversations happened. I imagined myself flying in a safe and secure place back home and the experience became quite enjoyable. The rear aerial gunner had the back gate open, allowing him to scan the regions we flew over. This gave me a front row seat to the scenery below. We flew over some beautiful areas, at one point we even passed over a huge lake of turquoise water surrounded by beautiful mountains.

We stopped in Tarin Kowt, also known as TK, to change helicopters to take us to the firebase where we would stage our MedCap. As soon as we and our pallet were unloaded from the Chinook, we were told there were some VIPs going with us on the next flight; therefore, we would have to leave the pallet behind and have it come in on the following flight. On the advice of the Doc, and a PA at KAF, I had thrown my aide bag and sleeping bag on it with the other medical supplies to lighten my load. As we parted from the pallet I hoped I hadn't made a mistake.

Once we arrived, I was pleased to see the friendly face of Don, who had left several days before. He got tasked to spend a couple of months with the team at the firebase and was also going to be a part of the MedCap. Apparently there was not an area directly on the firebase for the Chinooks to land so we were actually just outside the walls, close to an adjacent Dutch camp. Don and the team guys gathered us up on ATVs with our weapons and bags and set out on the dusty terrain toward the firebase where we would get assigned our rooms and a tour of the facility. When we got there, all the little Afghan boys gathered around me as if I were a celebrity.

Don noticed and explained, "They've never seen an American woman before."

I smiled and waved at my new fan club. They were really cute, and watching them giggle about me, I couldn't help but giggle back. I soon realized it was not only the little boys who were fascinated

THE "NO LIMIT" SOLDIER HAS LIMITS

by me, but the Afghanistan National Army (ANA) soldiers and adult men were just as curious. Their looks and giggles somehow weren't so endearing. I hurried past them, avoiding their gazes as much as possible.

As Don showed me around, I soon regretted the tour. The kitchen was, by far, the dirtiest I had ever seen and the moment I saw it I made the decision that I would live off of cereal and chips the entire time I was there. Then, just when I thought things couldn't be worse in regards to hygiene, he showed me our toilets. This firebase had not gotten plumbing installed for their latrines, and so we had the luxury of voiding into "shit burners," which were basically toilet seats with buckets under them that were emptied daily and the contents burned. When he opened a stall door to show me, the smell almost knocked me off of my feet. I would never take my bathroom at home for granted again. My room was filthy from the last person who stayed there, but I would clean it up easily.

"So Jenn, the initial plan for the MedCap was for it to be a one day trip," Don explained as I was getting settled in. "But now it looks like it's actually going to be two days."

"What does that mean?" I asked, almost knowing the answer.

"Just that we will be sleeping overnight in the field," he answered. This was news I was not prepared to hear and I instantly struggled with whether or not to let Greg know any further details. I didn't want him to worry any more than he already was.

"So, let me get this straight, Don; not one convoy to and from the site, but to site one, then to site two, sleeping in the field, and then back?" I asked.

He nodded and replied, "Actually, it could even be *three* days depending on the information we collect."

"Alright- got it," I said trying to swallow the lump of emotion welling up in my throat.

"Don't worry; everything will be fine and if anything happens, as long as you have your aide bag and narcotics for any casualties, you should be fine," he reassured.

Shortly after getting the news on the MedCap, we learned our pallet didn't make it. The soldier who stayed back to ensure it arrived apparently was unsure which pallet was ours and had them load the wrong one. The flights only came once a week, so that meant we were out of luck with our supplies. The team leader was informed of what happened and decided we would try to complete the MedCap with the medications they had already acquired on their firebase.

This meant that not only all of the hard work of preparing the medications and supplies loaded in the Pelican cases was for nothing, but my aide bag, narcotics, and my sleeping bag were all not coming either. After the extremely long day I had, and upon hearing bad news after bad news, I feared I was about to lose it. Up until this point in the deployment I had held it together. "Hey, are you ok?" Don asked, as I stared at the ceiling, trying with everything I had not to shed a tear.

"Yeah. I'm fine," I lied.

"Jenn, I see you are not fine. What's going on? What's wrong?" he asked.

I finally couldn't hold it back any longer and the tears began to flow down my face. "I'm scared to death of going out in this region on a convoy. Not to mention, since my supplies didn't make it, I have nothing I can use to treat patients if something happens out there. You just told me we are staying out in the field overnight and I don't even have a sleeping bag or pillow for the MedCap, let alone the next week." I felt like such a girl as I let my vulnerabilities show, but I couldn't shut off my emotions. I continued, "I come from such a sheltered background and this is not at all a typical Air Force deployment. Everything that is 'normal' and 'no big deal' to you is so unbelievably foreign to me."

"I have plenty of meds I can share with you and I have an extra sleeping bag and pillow you can use as long as you need it," he said understandingly. His words were comforting, especially considering his background – 27 years in Special Forces, witnessing things I couldn't even imagine. I hated to show any signs of weakness, filling the typical stereotype of a woman, but I had to admit that it helped to let it out.

THE "NO LIMIT" SOLDIER HAS LIMITS

"Listen," he reassured. "God forbid anything happens, but if it does, what I need you to do is get down and stay by me. I will do everything I can to make sure nothing happens to you."

"Thank you," I said. It was such a relief to hear him say that. I was so grateful for his kindness and willingness to take me and Becky under his wing. He didn't have to do the things he had, but I was so glad he did.

After I calmed down, he further explained the Green Berets to me. The teams I was augmenting were all stationed out of Ft. Bragg, NC and attached to various other groups. Each group deployed together on every cycle and when they were not deployed together, they trained together. The teams on the firebases were called Operational Detachment-Alphas (ODAs) and each team had been trained specifically for different types of missions. Some teams were specialized to deal with mountain warfare, combat diving, urban warfare, etc. Each of these teams consisted of twelve members with specific roles for the mission; however, they had all been cross-trained to be able to function in each other's tasks if something happened and one person was killed or unable to function in their job. The team commander usually had a Chief Warrant Officer as the assistant in command. There was the team sergeant, the intelligence sergeant, and then it was even further divided. There were ideally two team members in the following positions: the weapons sergeant, engineer sergeant, medic and the communications sergeant. Usually, of the two men in those positions, one was the senior who had at least one year of experience, while the second was a junior, often fresh out of training.

Having Don explain the structure of the team was helpful to give me more of an understanding of the people I was going to be working with over the next several months.

After our talk, Vance and Megan came and got us, and we went and took some pictures around the base and climbed the tower to look out into the surrounding villages. It was a beautiful evening. I stood on the tower, looking out into a farm, watching the Afghan children play with each other and chase a cow. The men were preparing to pray as they unrolled their prayer rugs and I found myself at peace for the first time that whole day. Despite everything that seemed to go wrong, I knew I was there for a reason and I wouldn't be there if I wasn't needed. So, I stood there and watched the children laugh for another thirty minutes before I finally went to sleep and put the day behind me.

CHAPTER **13**

Day 45
Preparing to Go

13 June 2008

We had a briefing early in the morning about our upcoming mission, which was now pushed back one day because the team commander decided our pallet was in fact a necessity, and so a truck was hired to bring our MedCap supplies from TK to us. This was a huge piece of good news in many ways. During the briefing, we also discussed the route and plan of action if we did, in fact, get into contact. I would be sitting in the back of the HMMWV, which meant if something happened my job was to duck; a job I was happy to take.

After the briefing, we picked up our supplies and began to separate everything we brought for the local nationals along with what the team already had into two piles, one for each day of the MedCap. I watched one of the team guys cutting up a bunch of pieces of an old parachute and tying the ends with cord, he saw me watching him,

"Hi there, I'm Chad," he said.

"Nice to meet you, what are you doing there?" I pointed to the pile of material in front of him.

"I'm taking this old parachute and making a hammock out of it. It beats sleeping on the ground out there…never know what may crawl into your sleeping bag and cuddle up next to ya," he laughed.

"Oh...um...yeah that's a good point," I pictured myself and my new friend, the huge camel spider, spooning. Chad must have seen my face.

"Would you like me to show you how to make one for yourself?" he asked.

"Please!" I smiled. Grateful for his help making the new bed I never would've imagined I needed. As we talked I learned he was actually another medic on the team. He seemed to love what he did and I felt we'd be able to work well together. Our preparation of supplies took several hours and once completed, we got our vehicles cleaned and ready to go.

Vance showed me how to operate the different weapons and how to reload them in case we came into contact. He was adamant our vehicle had any and every possible supply we might need, and that I knew where they all were. He wanted me to think of each and every scenario, to prepare for the worst. As he taught me about things to anticipate, I watched the other guys slowly wrap up their preps one by one, leaving us as the last vehicle to be deemed "ready." As I observed his attention to detail, I was comforted by having Vance on my truck because of his experience. We sat for a while together and he began to talk about some of the missions he was on the year before, which explained a lot about why he was the way he was.

"Well, last year was the hardest year of my life," he said. "I lost a very good friend and fellow medic in a TIC" (short for *Troops in Contact*).

"I'm so sorry," I said. "I understand if you don't want to talk about it."

"No, it's ok. I think it helps when I do," he replied.

"What happened?"

"During the TIC, he got shot in the arm and the bullet went through his armpit to his left chest, and he bled to death. I tried to stop it, but I couldn't. He died in my arms," he said.

It took a while before I was able to respond. "Vance, I can't begin to imagine what it must have felt like to have a friend, so close that

PREPARING TO GO

you called him your brother, die in your arms, and there was nothing you could do to stop it. I'm honored you shared this with me."

"No big deal. Like I said, I think it helps," he replied. "Last year was a very hard season for my team in Afghanistan; we were in TICs constantly, and each man on the team was driven to his very last drop of effort. It got so bad that at one point our team commander changed his whole focus from killing as many bad guys as we could to getting the rest of the members of our team home to our families *alive*."

"How awful," I said. I tried to understand the impact that would have on a person's psyche; having to continuously deal with tragedy, loss, and the unknown of who the next casualty would be.

"After last year," he continued, "I went through some very difficult times adjusting to normal life."

"How so?" I asked.

"I would sit on the floor in my room and stare into space for hours at a time, thinking. I withdrew from friends and family and handled my pain in the only way I knew how; by myself," he confessed.

"How did you get through it?" I asked.

"I don't really know. I was eventually able to pull myself out of my depression, but I'm still not the same person I was before last year."

I could see the pain and anger behind his eyes and I believed what he said earlier was true; having someone listen to what he was feeling was therapeutic for him. He explained that with everything he saw and did last year, he developed a fear of missions.

"So then why did you volunteer to go on this MedCap?" I asked.

"I had to get over my fear and address my inner devils face to face," he explained.

We talked about family and he told me he had a son. "Would you let him join the military?" I asked.

"HELL NO! I've sacrificed everything short of my own life several times over for this country, and I have more than paid my own and my family's debt to society. My son is going to live the life I gave up so that he could." I gave him a hug and thanked him genuinely for sharing his story.

After lunch we took the vehicles out to the heavy weapons range to test fire the weapons on the HMMWV prior to our departure. I got to fire the MRK-19 (an automatic grenade launcher pronounced *Mark-19*), the .50 cal, and the M240 machine gun. My favorite was the MRK-19; it was really neat to get the chance to fire those weapons, something I likely would never get the opportunity to experience again. As we were out there, letting each vehicle test fire, I saw an Afghan man slowly approaching us. I felt a sense of fear bubbling up inside.

"Hey Chad, you see that guy walking towards us?" I pointed. "Is he something we should be concerned about?"

"Don't worry Lt., he's a regular," Chad said.

"Oh yeah, that guy?" Travis, another guy on the team, confirmed. "He comes out to pick up the brass so he can sell it at the bazaar."

I thought it was so sad he had to do that just so he could get a few cents to help feed his family. I waved him over to our vehicle and handed him a handful of the casings on our truck. He nodded and waved a "thank you" and I smiled and waved; it was the least I could do.

When we returned to base, I had a couple of patients waiting for me at the clinic. One was a little boy who had a dog bite on his ear and another was one of the cooks who had acid reflux. After I treated them I went to watch the ANA and the team guys play volleyball. As I watched the game with Megan, we couldn't help but notice the spectators seemed to turn their attention from the game to us.

"Jenn, look at that. Can you believe this?" Megan asked.

"What is it?" I asked.

"Look at their cameras," she said.

I looked closely and saw that the ANA guys actually had their cameras pointed in our direction, filming *us* for the majority of the game. At first it was funny, but over time it was both annoying and unnerving. We tried to ignore it, but it got to be too much. I looked at Megan and said, "You know what? Give me that." I grabbed her camera out of her hands and pointed it right back at them. "What do you think about that!" I yelled, "How does that feel?" Megan and I laughed at our small, yet effective stance.

Sure enough, once they realized what we were doing, they got the message and stopped filming us. After the game was over we decided to play a match; minus the spectators of course.

CHAPTER **14**

Days 47 & 48
The MedCap

15 and 16 June 2008

 We woke up at 0100 hours to get everything together with a goal to leave by 0300. As I loaded my things into the back of the HMMWV, I looked up at the night sky and realized how beautifully clear it was. The stars were brilliant and breathtaking. I found the Cancer constellation and realized my birthday was soon approaching. I couldn't believe a year had already almost passed from last summer.

 As I stared up at the stars, I felt an overwhelming sense of peace. I felt closeness to God on a completely different level then I had ever experienced. As I stood there, I began to pray; asking not for protection, but for the strength to accept whatever my fate may be. I found myself truly accepting the fact I may not come home. I never thought I would feel such acceptance; for the first time in my life I realized I had no control of the circumstances to come; it was in God's hands. I felt a sense of peace in that moment of realization, a peace that only surfaces when there is a true understanding of life's circumstances being so much bigger than ourselves.

 As Megan and I loaded our things we had a conversation I never wanted to have again.

THE MEDCAP

"If something happens to me Jenn, I want to tell you that my wedding ring is in the top pocket of my backpack," she said.

"Ok... Mine is in my journal, under my pillow," I said.

"All of my stuff is still packed for the most part, back in my room at the firebase," she continued.

"Mine too," I replied. "Um, Megan... If something *does* happen out there... I...uh... I would want you to tell..." As I tried to tell her what I wanted her to pass on to my Greg, I couldn't hold back my tears. She was very sweet, and since I couldn't get the words out, she spoke for me.

"You know what I would tell him? I would tell him how I feel like I know him because of how much you talk about him, and how it is so obvious how much you love him and how much of a part of you he is."

I nodded in thanks, reassured what she just said was exactly what I would want him to know if anything happened to me. After we finished talking we sat together in the darkness holding hands and said another prayer. It was nice having her there; after our moment together I again felt a sense of peace with whatever may be. After everything was loaded, we ate and then got all of our body armor and gear on and headed out of the safety of the gates and into the night of the unknown.

Sitting in the back of the HMMWV was kind of like sitting in the bed of a pickup truck, except of course, that the sides of the vehicle we were in were bullet proof and we had a .50 cal machine gun sitting over our heads. As we sat, and waited for the ANA trucks to join in the convoy, the team commander came over to my truck and whispered in my ear; "Jenn, promise me, if *anything* happens you will *get down*. There is nothing you will be able to do in your position with your M4, so please, just get down."

"Ok, I will," I promised without difficulty.

"Ok guys, get your NODs (short for night optical device, also commonly referred to as night vision goggles) on and pick a side of the terrain, I need you to be scanning for anything unusual," Vance instructed from above. He would be the turret gunner manning the .50 cal for our vehicle.

As we pulled our night vision goggles on I said, "I'll take the east, what do I need to be watching for?"

"Look in the crevasses and along the horizon for any enemy activity. They often ambush from positions in this type of terrain," he answered. I couldn't believe I was really doing this. All of the scenario training I had participated in the previous years, that I never thought I would use, suddenly all came back to me.

Our convoy was quite impressive; it was comprised of six HMMWVs and ten additional trucks driven by the ANA, which carried the supplies for the MedCap. The fact that it was so large and our vehicle was somewhat in the middle was comforting. However this comfort was short-lived. Every vehicle drove blacked out; meaning we traveled in darkness without headlights. To avoid being seen by insurgents we relied on our night vision goggles to observe our surroundings. Suddenly, out of nowhere, the ANA truck that was behind our vehicle turned its headlights on, completely illuminating our vehicle for the world to see. Vance about lost his mind as he screamed into the radio, "What the hell are you doing? Turn off your fucking lights!" We were a sitting duck, a perfect target, had someone been searching for one. We braced ourselves for any and everything. Finally after seconds, which felt like hours, the truck lights turned off. I never knew why they turned them on, but I couldn't avoid my suspicions that it was intentional. I had been told by others that sometimes the enemy would infiltrate the ranks of the ANA. I hoped that was not the case with any of the soldiers I encountered, but it kept me on guard.

We drove on and off the road, up and down hills and narrow passes and past the occasional compounds for about an hour before we came to the edge of the Green Zone. Up until that point we had been driving in desert, the Green Zone was marked by trees and vegetation which made the area dangerous due to more strategic fighting positions for the enemy.

THE MEDCAP

By the time we got there, the sun had already begun to rise and I could see farmers and their children gathering in front of their homes to watch us. I wondered what they must have been thinking, seeing us pass by with our massive convoy, weapons and gear. Looking down into the Green Zone I could see the Helmand River, which runs through a good portion of southern Afghanistan. It is known for the violence associated with the Taliban due to all of the poppy fields growing around it that were used to fund their operations. To get to our final destination for Day One of our MedCap we had to ford across the river. As we got closer Vance yelled down, "Hey! You guys need to scan the rocks and riverbed! It's early morning and this is a prime time for an ambush to occur."

I could feel my heart pounding and my fingers tighten around my weapon as I looked at all the rocks and caves as potential hiding places. Just to my right was a huge mountain that had on its peak a castle that was built by Alexander the Great. In any other scenario, I would have loved to get a closer look at it, but as we passed through the dangerous area, I was consumed with my duty of looking for enemy activity.

As our vehicle got closer to the river, I watched the trucks ahead of us begin to cross the water; thank God the ANA already had the other side secured. Our vehicle made the journey with no problems and once we were all across, we stopped on the river bank for "chai," which was a tea Afghans traditionally drank. At first I was skeptical, mainly because of the water it was made with, but the team guys put my mind at ease saying they had partaken in chai many times before and had not suffered any illness. I tried it and was quite surprised at how good it tasted. It was a nice break, and peaceful watching the sun rise over the mountains. As I sat there, I realized what a beautiful country it was. Sadly, the horrible things that happened here made it hard to appreciate the natural beauty.

After our break, we pressed on for another forty minutes until we reached the compound where we would have the MedCap. I'm not sure what I was expecting it to be, but I was not prepared for what we saw. It was a building made of mud, like all of the other compounds we saw along the way, with no electricity or plumbing. The floors were covered with straw that was saturated with urine and feces, both human and animal. I found the most "private" appearing room I could to set up as my exam room. I made an exam table out of a litter and four MRE (meals ready to eat) boxes to hold the litter up off the ground. I set my box of medicine off to the side and my other supplies on a shelf that was carved out of the wall. We would see the patients with an interpreter because the locals in the region either spoke Pashto (the same language spoken in Pakistan and typically used by members of the Taliban) or Dari, a language used less often by the Taliban.

Four of us would be treating patients; I was the only female. The others were the two medics (Vance and Chad), an Afghan doctor, and Don, my fellow PA. I was there for the women, but I was anticipating a low turnout if any at all based on the briefing before we left.

"Don't expect many female patients, their husbands rarely allow them to leave the homes," Don had said. This forecast could not have been more wrong. There were at least two hundred women that came in the morning alone. Up to then, I had not seen any local women and now they were flowing in. It was heartbreaking to examine them; they were all covered in filth, their teeth were falling out, and they had to cover their faces when in public. I think what struck me the most about them was the sadness I saw in their eyes. I could see how tired they were from the poverty stricken lives they had led.

The condition of the men and children wasn't much better. Most of the children didn't have shoes and if they did they were falling apart. Hundreds of people showed up and their complaints were all the same: body aches, belly pain, headaches, colds, and fevers. Every once in a while I would see something different, but the majority was all the same. Women often complained of the symptoms of their "monthly sickness" and their babies dying shortly after birth, which was most likely due to malnutrition and dehydration. I had never seen patients before in a situation where we didn't speak the same language. Relying on the interpreter to translate what the patients were actually complaining of, and then my instructions on how to take the medications I prescribed or specific lifestyle changes they could make to improve their conditions was challenging. I realized very quickly how much I had underestimated the importance of being able to speak directly to patients. With my patients back home, I could pick up on a tone of voice and body language much easier, which was so important in deciphering if what was being said was the whole story or not. I could watch their reactions to what I said and could see whether they understood or whether I needed to explain things more appropriately. In this situation, it was all a guessing game, a frustrating one at that.

Late in the morning I saw the two patients I will never forget. The first was a three-month-old infant girl who was so malnourished she looked like a newborn. She was deathly ill from severe dehydration. The child was lethargic and her skin turgor was unbelievable; I could pinch her skin, and instead of it bouncing back like well hydrated skin, hers stayed tented up for several seconds before returning back to her body. Her tongue was sticking out because she was trying to suckle food and it was as dry as her fragile skin. Her respirations were extremely labored and fast and I knew that this child would die if she did not get treatment. We had IV equipment, but not small enough catheters for a baby. I searched and found a 25 gauge needle and managed to get venous access and got some fluid in, but since I didn't have a catheter, any movement could potentially rupture the vessel. As I tried to secure the needle, that is exactly what happened; the needle was moved and it punctured the wall of the vein. Just like that, I lost the venous access. I tried again on her other arm, and was unsuccessful. I gave her the rest of the fluid bolus through her rectum and arranged for a medevac to get the baby and her mother to a hospital where she could get more definitive care. As I explained the plan to the mother via my interpreter, I saw a look of fear come over her face as she shook her head. She explained if she went without notifying her husband, he would kill her. I could not believe what I was hearing. I tried to explain to her that if she didn't take her baby to the hospital, she would surely die within the next day or two. She nodded her understanding, but insisted on talking with her husband before doing anything. She promised to come back after talking to him. She never did, and I never saw her again.

After realizing the woman would not go on the medevac, I went down to tell the Captain the news. As soon as I walked back into the compound I saw the excitement was far from over. Apparently while I was making the arrangements for the baby, one of the Afghan soldiers came running up to Megan carrying a girl over his shoulder, no more than fourteen years old, who was gasping for each breath and moaning in pain. Her husband had hit her over the head with a shovel and pushed her off of the roof in anger, resulting in her falling over twenty feet. Thankfully the Afghanistan National Police (ANP) already had him in custody when they brought her to us.

By the time I came back to the exam room, she was unconscious and unresponsive lying on the litter soaked in urine, indicating she had lost control of her bladder; a bad sign in a fall victim. After a quick assessment, Don and I quickly determined her status to be critical. We intubated her and applied a c-collar. We established two IV lines and called for a medevac; we did not have the means to do much for her in that environment and our supply of sedative drugs was very limited. It took about thirty minutes for the bird to land, and by that time her medications were wearing off and she began to aspirate. Her spontaneous respirations were causing me to be unsuccessful in ventilating her. She vomited, forcing me to extubate her (pull the breathing tube out of her throat) to prevent her from choking to death. As we carried her on the liter up the hill I realized the adrenaline was starting to wear off and my body's fatigue was settling in. Thankfully the medevac arrived when it did and I relayed the information to the accepting medic informing him that he would need to re-intubate her. As we watched them load her into the helicopter I felt overwhelming sadness for the young girl. I later found out that she was the niece of the head of the ANP, which was a huge deal. We were reassured that her husband was dealt with "the Afghan way." Several days later I was informed of the diagnosis of a severe intracranial hemorrhage and she was brain dead, being kept alive by a ventilator. The staff waited for her family to arrive and then eventually they discontinued life support. This was the first patient under my care who had died.

By the end of the day I was exhausted, mentally and physically. We had a meal, waited for the sun to go down, and loaded the trucks again to travel to the site of the following day's MedCap. We traveled for about an hour and a half, which seemed like eternity. Every several feet along the way there was a detail that walked alongside our vehicles scanning the sides of the road with metal detectors and bomb dogs in search of IEDs. It seemed that we would never arrive at the next compound. I was struggling the whole journey to keep my eyes open, but I knew I had to stay awake to scan the terrain.

Once we arrived, we hung the parachute hammocks we made between two vehicles, I was profoundly grateful Chad helped me make mine.

"Not too shabby huh?" Chad smiled as he helped me hang mine.

"Thank you again for helping me," I said. He smiled and nodded.

"Yep, these things are a must-have out here." Travis said as he walked by, "I've slept on the ground before and believe me, this is much better." My vision of the large camel spider crawling in my sleeping bag with me returned. I smiled and we resumed our preparation to rest overnight.

Shortly thereafter I did a quick baby wipe bath and went to sleep. All through the night we heard roosters crowing, dogs barking, and donkeys moaning. The team guys alternated every hour for security duty and each time they changed personnel I heard the previous guy wake up his relief. I got three to four hours of interrupted sleep at the most.

When I awoke, I had to go to the bathroom, only to find there was no "bathroom" for me to go to. There was no door to close or shelter to retreat to; there wasn't even a tree to squat under. Megan and I, being the only females, had to "improvise". We took a piece of the parachute we'd used the night before and took turns holding it over each other while we handled our business.

When we returned to the vehicles, I tried to brush my hair and wipe down with baby wipes again. I was absolutely covered in dirt; "dusty" was an understatement. I couldn't even get a comb through my hair; it was completely filled with dirt. I decided the best option was to tie it up in the scarf I had been using to keep the dirt out of my mouth when we traveled. As we took in our surroundings, and became accustomed to our treatment area, we realized we had no building to see patients in and in anticipation of the hot midday sun we improvised by draping parachute material over the compound wall, securing it to the trucks for shade. After this experience I had a whole new respect for the parachute and its many uses....hammock, canopy of shade, and most importantly, a bathroom door.

If my "camping trip" wasn't enough, today was Father's Day and I couldn't get Greg out of my mind. I wanted to talk to him so badly and Don must have sensed my feelings because, without saying a word, he brought me a satellite phone.

"Here, call your husband."

"Wow, I don't know what to say...thank you," I said in disbelief. He handed me the phone and walked away. I found a quiet spot and dialed the phone number. As soon as I heard his voice I felt the lump forming in my throat. I missed him so much. I couldn't tell him what I was doing or where I was. He had no idea I had just traveled through a very dangerous part of the country in the back of a HMMWV, loaded a fourteen year old girl onto a helicopter knowing her chances of survival were slim to none, witnessed a mother turn down care for her dying baby because she was scared for her own life, or that I spent the night in the field.

I knew eventually I would tell him what I did, but it was not going to be anytime soon. I had never kept anything from him and it was tearing me apart.

"Happy Father's Day sweetie," I knew he was missing little Griffen terribly.

"Thanks Nej, I wish you were here, I miss you so much. How are things going?" he asked.

"Oh, you know…the typical deployment stuff…just another day," I lied. I fought to hold back the tears as I put up the charade to spare him from worry.

"Well, you are a 'Medic Warrior' after all, so try to stay out of trouble while you take on the bad guys," he said with what I imagine as a shit eating grin on his face. Greg could always make me smile. Hearing him joke innocently helped me to feel the sense of home I needed. It gave me the energy I needed to start the day. We talked for a few more short minutes and then it was back to reality.

The morning was filled with patients, but not nearly as many as the first day. I saw two more really sick babies who were twins. I was successful in arranging transportation for them to the Dutch hospital nearby for treatment and later talked to the accepting physician who informed me one had a case of meningitis and the other was severely dehydrated.

The patient that stood out the most to me the second day was a boy I estimated to be around the age of fourteen or fifteen. He was different from the other locals. While all the other patients were filthy and wearing rags and sandals that showed worn and leathered feet from endless hours in the fields, he was neatly groomed, with nice, clean feet, soft hands and brand new appearing black clothes. It was evident he came from money and the fact that he was dressed in all black and appeared the way he did made us all highly suspicious he was involved with the Taliban in one way or another. The Captain instantly honed in on this and separated him from the rest of the people for further questioning. Unfortunately we didn't get much information from him, other than an admission that if he had to choose between fighting with the ANA and Coalition forces or the Taliban, he would fight with the latter, because they were Muslim and we weren't. It sickened me that we had to let him go, especially seeing it written all over his face, and in his smirk, that he was one of them. I was somewhat reassured in knowing that at least we had a way of identifying him in the future if need be.

The morning quickly passed, and before we knew it, it was lunchtime. As we were all beginning to take note of our bodies reminding us of our hunger; we saw an elderly man with a long white beard with resolute eyes dressed in all white slowly approaching us. The Captain saw him and they instantly embraced in a friendly hug. The man proceeded to shake all of our hands...apparently he was an ANA commander for the troops in that region. As we sat and listened to him and the Captain talk, we learned he was a man who had an internal hatred for the Taliban and what they did to his family. Several of his cousins and brothers had been imprisoned for years for resisting them. He had accomplished much in the war against the Taliban and we discovered by listening to him talk, what a great asset he was to the Coalition forces. He brought us all lunch and was very receptive to everyone. It was an interesting and memorable encounter; I was impressed with his candor and support for us. He took pride in his people and the country he loved before the Taliban regime.

After we ate, we loaded up the rest of our gear and began our journey back to the base. It was broad daylight and as we pulled out of the compound it became very apparent to me how "on edge" I was about being in a daylight convoy. As we traveled through several small villages, I saw children running up to the street to wave as we passed by. Many held out their hands hoping for food or anything we might throw. I later found out that was a tactic the Taliban often used to distract the people in a convoy; while they were paying attention to the children on one side of the road, they would ambush from the opposite. It was intense traveling through each village, but there were some that were more unnerving than others. The narrow streets and crowds of people surrounded us, forcing our convey to move at an uncomfortably slow pace. High cliffs and buildings on both sides of the road were ideal staging locations for an ambush. We had no place to go; we were sitting ducks. Vance was on high alert as he manned the .50 cal.

At one point he saw a man on the corner of the street with a cell phone which could have easily been a remote detonator for an IED. Vance quickly pointed his weapon at him.

"Someone tell me differently, because I am about two seconds from opening fire on this guy!" he screamed into the radio.

"Stand down! Stand down! Stand down!" the Captain responded, "He's with us! He's ANP! I repeat, he's with us."

"Roger that," Vance replied and eased off the weapon.

I felt nauseous with fear and came very close to throwing up. I tried not to think about what would have happened if he had fired, but the thoughts remained.

As we were leaving the last village before we arrived at the river, I looked back at the people and noticed several men dressed in all black with black turbans staring back at us with pure hatred in their eyes. They had no idea I was a woman due to my helmet, sunglasses and the scarf over my face to keep the dust out of my nose and mouth. I looked at the men with an unease that was indescribable. About three or four of them stopped walking and gathered in the middle of the street standing and watching. I felt those eyes staring directly at me, wanting me dead. As the distance between us became larger, I couldn't look away, watching them as they watched us.

After two days of being covered from head to toe in dirt, traveling in 125 degree weather in our full body armor, and utterly exhausted, we were in a unique state of mind. Once we got to the river, we decided it was absolutely necessary to take a quick dip. I would have *never* gotten in that water before, but I was so hot and so dirty I couldn't wait to jump in. As soon as I did, I dipped my head in the water and got my hair wet which felt incredible. Something so simple was such a big deal at that point, I was refreshed and happy. However, as I came up from under the water I looked up and saw a large piece of human feces float right by me. Me in my right mind would have likely screamed in disgust and raced to get out of the water and promptly dry heaved on the riverbank, but after what we had been exposed to over the last two days, that part of me was long gone. Out of desperation we all remained in the cool water and for thirty minutes we played like children in the dirtiest river I had ever seen. It certainly made me appreciate the old cliché'; "Desperate times call for desperate measures". As I continued to enjoy the cool water, I made a mental note to make sure I took a hefty dose of an antibiotic when I got back to the base.

After we had enough, we loaded up and finished the rest of the trip back. I couldn't have been happier to see that American flag flying high as we approached base and as we entered the gate I breathed a deep sigh of relief.

CHAPTER **15**

Day 49
Happy Anniversary

17 June 2008

Two years ago was the happiest day of my life. It was the day I married my best friend. I could hardly believe the time had passed as quickly as it had; it seemed like yesterday I was walking down the aisle to the man I loved with all of my heart. As I sat and reminisced, I found myself saddened I couldn't be with Greg on our day. When people are together every day, we lose sight of how special it is to be together. The little things that seemed so annoying about each other were what I missed the most. I couldn't stand this thing he did with his pinky toe or how he had to have his Harley Davidson t-shirts washed a special way. I drove him crazy by never screwing on lids tightly and always losing my keys and ID card. I missed singing to each other on the phone, or in the shower, our silly little games, holding hands, playing cards....I missed everything about him.

He sent me an anniversary card that I read over and over. We had been apart before, and we did just fine, but that didn't make it any easier to be away. I am not "that person" who can leave for months and months at a time, over and over again, for the job—my life is my family and I didn't want to leave him again. I knew that wherever he was on that day, and whatever he was doing, he was carrying a piece of me with him and I carried him with me. My Gerg was the reason I became the person I was; he made me want to be better.

To my Gerg, from 7,000 miles away…Happy Anniversary, I love you with all that I am.

CHAPTER **16**

Days 53-57
Working with the FST

21-25 June 2008

I left the team I was with, along with Don, Megan and Vance and flew back to KAF on June 18th, and I found myself alone. I had formed some friendships through the experience of the MedCap and was sad to part ways, but eager to reunite with Becky. I was supposed to catch a ring flight (which was a weekly itinerary flown by a Chinook to the firebases) to my firebase on the 20th. I got all of my belongings packed and on the pallet as directed. I waited on the flight line to board the Chinook in my body armor, gloves, helmet, weapons and eye protection, ready to face whatever was in store for me at my new home. After what I had just experienced, the thought of another ride in a Chinook in Afghanistan was not nearly as intimidating.

As I waited I looked up and I saw the flight line NCO walking toward me shaking his head and I knew it was not a good situation. He informed me I was not going to be able to get on the bird because one of the two Chinooks that were going to be making the journey was broken down and the other was filled with pallets; therefore, there was no room. Filled with pallets? Wait a second...my *stuff* is on one of those pallets. Luckily I had a backpack with all of my necessary items on my person. The majority of my things would be arriving long before me since the ring flights only go out to the firebases once a week. I was so disappointed, I wanted to get to where I was going and get settled. I also was not looking forward to spending another week in Kandahar.

As I was walking back to the truck I noticed I was not alone; there were about five other people in the same boat. As we shared in our disappointment, I began to talk to a guy named Jay, who just so happened to be one of the SF guys who was based out of TK (Tarin Kowt), which is the first stop on the ring flight. He offered to get me on a fixed wing flight the next morning that was going to TK, and even though he couldn't promise me a flight out of there, it was still a no-brainer. I could sit at KAF for another week doing nothing, or I could go to TK and see something new. In addition to getting me out of KAF, it would also give me a chance to work with the Forward Surgical Team (FST) whom I had met at BAF while I waited for the next ring flight. I quickly thanked him and accepted the invitation, and at 0500 hours on the morning of the 21st I was on my way to TK.

Once I arrived, I was greeted by the airfield crew who grabbed my bag and helped me to a room that Jay was nice enough to have arranged for my stay. And it was not just any room, but nothing less than the VIP room in the SF section of the camp; I was very grateful. Once I got my things secured, I went over to the FST clinic to say hello. I was happy to see them all again and even though I only met them briefly at BAF, they seemed like a good group of people.

My early assessment was accurate. As soon as I walked in, they greeted me with friendly hellos and were more than happy to let me jump in and get my hands dirty. They had been very busy, doing over forty-five surgeries in the two weeks they had been there. So they didn't get burned-out, they switched off with the Dutch camp on receiving trauma patients every other week. When not doing trauma cases in the Operating Room (OR) they would see Sick Call for the local nationals. The clinic was always full of patients who were there for follow-up care, sent from other firebases nearby, or people who just came on their own accord.

WORKING WITH THE FST

When I was there they had a lot of pediatric cases, which were all related to orthopedic injuries and were often bone infections and fractures due to "falling out of trees" or some other excuse. Some patients were also there for gunshot wounds. The team had just operated on a lady the day before who had a cesarean section at the local hospital that turned out to be a makeshift hysterectomy. The "surgeon" left half of her uterus and cervix, cut her ureters and slashed her bladder in three places. Luckily the FST was able to put her back together, but she had a long recovery ahead of her. That was just one example of the type of medical care local nationals received by their fellow countrymen.

One little girl that came in had pus draining from her hip for several months and her father *finally* decided to bring her in for treatment. When I saw her, I thought she was no more than four years old, but I was told she was at least ten; it was like looking at a skeleton with skin. She also had a severe scolotic curve of her thoracic spine that was bent forward 100°. It was amazing she didn't have any respiratory difficulty due to the deformity. Her hip x-ray revealed the femoral head was almost completely gone due to the chronic infection eating it away. The only thing we could do for her was take her to surgery every day and irrigate her bone extensively and keep her on antibiotics. I felt so bad for her. She was the patient I dealt with the most and luckily by the time I left she was doing much better, but still not out of the woods.

I also met a very interesting nurse and interpreter, who worked for the Coalition Forces, named Suraya. She was born in Afghanistan and moved to the United States in 1980 before Russia and the Taliban moved in to the country. I had several conversations with her and found her to be quite fascinating. I asked her opinion about what had happened to her country; specifically the women. She replied, "I am absolutely disgusted." She went on to tell me about how happy her life was when she was growing up.

"Jennifer, I never wore a burka. I was educated; I had a profession and respect." She showed me pictures of her in high school on a volleyball team, photos from her wedding and various other stages in her life. I was amazed to see the images which reflected how the culture of this country had so drastically changed from that to what it was now. It was heartbreaking. I couldn't imagine how I would feel if the same shift happened in America. I couldn't imagine what it must have been like for her to return to a place she once called a happy home that was now filled with such hatred and poverty. As we talked further, I discovered she lived in Santa Cruz, California, the same city my Aunt Jane had lived in for many years. I exchanged emails with her and promised to put her in touch with Jane. I wished she could travel with me to the firebase, but I was happy to have had the short time with her that I did, she offered a rare perspective.

In the week I was at TK, Don and the team from the MedCap surprisingly stopped in while they were out on a mission. One of their vehicles had mechanical problems, forcing them to get it repaired at TK before they could continue. I was so happy to see them. In the short time I spent with them, I had grown very fond of them and made a lot of good friends. I spent the majority of my time there with Chad and Travis, whom I had befriended the most on the MedCap. It was profound how quickly friendships were formed out in the middle of "Nowhere Afghanistan." Right before I left their firebase they had begun to prepare for a very dangerous and potentially violent mission. After I said goodbye to them, I found myself frequently worrying about their safety. I gave Travis a hug as soon as I saw them and told him how worried I'd been.

He looked at me and smiled. "We do it because we love it; don't worry about us."

"Well, excuse me, Mr. Tough Guy," I said. He smiled.

The night before they left, Chad, Travis and I laughed for a good half-hour in the dining hall as we debated about strawberries and bananas. We were trying to decide which fruit looked more "ridiculous" for a Green Beret to eat. Before we went to bed that night we all hugged goodbye and they left early the next morning.

The day after they left I walked into the clinic only to discover a

WORKING WITH THE FST

group of people, mainly involving the ANA had been ambushed and came to the FST for help. One was shot in the back; another had a through-and-through gunshot wound to his thigh that destroyed his penis as it exited. The last patient was shot in the abdomen and his stomach was destroyed along with some of his large bowel.

Thankfully all three patients were stabilized and were expected to do just fine. As I walked out of the OR, after the last case, I saw another Afghan man lying on a liter with agonal breathing, which is what occurs just prior to death. Apparently he was a detainee who fell and had a severe head injury. There was nothing left to do for him but let him die and eventually that was what he did.

I couldn't help but stand there next to him, watching him slowly dying and wondering who he was and what he had done to people before he was captured; it gave me chills. He was likely a man who killed and stood over many innocent people and watched them die, and now he was slowly fading away in a treatment facility where many of his victims were treated. It was ironic to say the least. Because he was a detainee and a member of the Taliban, since he died under our care an autopsy was requested. I was looking forward to seeing it since I had never been a part of one before, but unfortunately it was performed the morning I left TK.

I enjoyed my week with the FST. I learned a lot and would have loved to stay the rest of my deployment with them, but I knew I had a much bigger purpose elsewhere, and elsewhere I went.

CHAPTER 17

Day 58
Arrival at the Firebase

26 June 2008

After two months I couldn't believe I finally arrived at the firebase I was assigned to; the deployment was a third of the way over! As the Chinook landed on the helicopter landing zone (HLZ), it was so nice to see Becky out there waiting for me. We ran to each other and hugged. We'd been separated for almost three weeks and it felt so nice to have her back. As I got my things set in my room, Becky and Hal, the junior medic, showed me around the base. They pointed to an empty spot next to the rooms which was where the dining facility used to be. Just before Becky's arrival, the dining facility burned down due to a gas leak, so they were relying on local nationals who worked on the base to prepare their food; this was not good news for my digestive system. They guided me to the bathrooms we would be sharing with all of the guys.

Hal explained the rules, "Here's the bathroom and showers, I have designated a thirty minute time for 'female showers' every day, meaning the door can be locked and the guys will stay out. The rest of the day you are welcome to the facility, but you are on your own when it comes to privacy."

"There is no more modesty after being here for any amount of time," Becky added.

ARRIVAL AT THE FIREBASE

As we walked through the bathroom I could see what they were talking about. The stalls were made of thin aluminum walls; therefore, privacy was not something that would be easy to come by. When I looked down at the toilet, I saw porn magazines lying on the back of it. No privacy indeed.

"Sorry about that," Hal apologized, clearly embarrassed. "You're living with a bunch of men."

"No problem, I get it," I said quickly, ready to move on to the next part of the tour.

I was a little uneasy to say the least when I saw the location of the clinic. It was right on the outer edge of the firebase and when I opened the door to where the patients would come in I was literally looking out into the local area. The only thing separating us from "them" was some concertina wire (c-wire) and a security checkpoint armed with ANA soldiers.

Once I got past the location and focused on the actual clinic itself, I must say I was impressed. It had tiled floors, four treatment bays, a pharmacy, supply room and a portable x-ray machine. There was no lab capability, but there was a glucometer and urine dipsticks for very basic workups. As I looked through the supplies, I realized I would have limitations on what I could do for the patients I saw. The way I had been taught to evaluate patients was with many more resources, such as a lab, radiology, and specialists just a phone call away. I would have to make do with what I had. Just as we did during the MedCap, we would see the patients with an interpreter, also known as a "Terp". I met the Terp I would work with most often, his name was IG (pronounced "eye gee").

While I was in the clinic we saw a few patients, which gave me a chance to work with Hal for the first time. As we did assessments and physical exams of the patients, I could see his thought processes and understand his training background. He had a strong knowledge on how to manage trauma patients, but admitted basic skills with medical management. With each patient we treated he was eager to learn from me, while I appreciated his experience as well. I felt we would be able to work together and complement each other well.

Once the clinic closed we resumed the tour of my new home for the next several months. Hal explained the firebase was once a Taliban headquarters we overtook in 2002. It was eerie to think I was standing in the same buildings that were once occupied by such malicious people. As we walked, one of the guys came out wearing no shirt, and a pair of "Ranger panties" which were very short shorts the guys were issued for physical training.

"Hello ladies," he smirked as he strutted by us.

"What the *hell* are you doing man?" Hal said, "How about you show some respect dude? Go put some clothes on."

"My bad Hal! I didn't know they were out here," the team guy said as he continued on his way to the gym. Becky and I looked at each other and smiled.

"Sorry ladies, that was completely unacceptable. The guys aren't used to having a female presence out here, but I will make sure they treat you with respect," Hal said apologetically.

"Thanks," we said. It was nice to know he cared. I knew Greg and Mike, Becky's husband, would appreciate someone like Hal looking out for us.

Hal dropped me off at the Operations Center (OpCen) where I met Ivan, the intelligence sergeant. He took me up to the roof and pointed to all of the surrounding villages and told me they were all filled with hostile forces, with the exception of one. He instructed me on how to ask basic questions, in order to gather intelligence from the patients I would be treating in the clinic. "You'd be surprised what you can get out of people by just asking such basic things," he said.

"I never would've imagined," I acknowledged, as I took note of what he said. He explained this region had been a Taliban safe-haven for many years and just recently we had gotten control over it. So, naturally there were still a lot of locals who supported our opposition.

"Expect the firebase to get attacked on an almost daily basis. Usually it's not that big of a deal, but I want you to be prepared," Ivan continued to explain.

ARRIVAL AT THE FIREBASE

I thought of the conversation I had with Bob back at BAF, telling me we may be asked to assist the team if we got attacked. "What do we need to do when that happens?" I asked.

"The biggest help you guys can give us is manning the radios and the camera while we take a wall. Sometimes you can locate the insurgents on the camera and you can call the coordinates to the mortar pit."

"Ok, got it," I replied. Everything I had been told in preparation for coming there had been true. All of the strange looks and the "They're sending _you_ there?" comments we got back at Bagram, when we told people where we were going suddenly made perfect sense. I could feel goose bumps on my arms.

After my briefing with Ivan, I met the senior medic, Kyle, and instantly got bad vibes from him. He came across as arrogant and overly confident, which is a dangerous combination in medicine. He hadn't been feeling well, apparently due to eating the food prepared by the local cooks.

"I'm sorry to hear you aren't feeling well, what are your symptoms?" I asked.

"Well, obviously I have gastroenteritis. I have generalized abdominal pain and intermittent episodes of diarrhea," he explained with extreme confidence.

"That sucks, how long have you been suffering from it?"

"It's been a full twenty four hours, pretty serious stuff," he said, "I am just finally getting over the worst of it. Pretty much everyone here has had the same symptoms."

"Do you know if everyone is washing their hands? Poor hygiene can make things like this turn in to a widespread problem," I offered.

"Of course I thought of that!" he snapped.

"Great, I am glad you did. Have you gone to the kitchen where the food is being prepared to see if there is an obvious reason why this is happening with everyone?"

"You have no idea how things go out here, I have it under control," he scowled. He was very territorial and didn't want me or anyone else coming in and telling him how to run *his* show.

"I'm glad you're taking care of it," I said, as I walked away feeling a discomfort in my gut that was not at all due to the food...this guy was not going to be easy to get along with.

About an hour after meeting him I was in my room unpacking, when he came in with a "patient" for me. The patient was of course complaining of diarrhea, like everyone else, so I asked him all of the alarm questions which, if positive, would lead me to believe it was a bacterial infection requiring treatment with antibiotics, instead of the typical viral or toxin-induced diarrhea. When all of his answers were negative and he looked fine, I offered him symptomatic treatment and educated him on proper hydration and letting it run its course.

Shortly after the patient left I realized I had been set up. During the time I was talking with the patient, Kyle decided he would "critique" my work. A nationally certified Physician Assistant was being "evaluated" by a medic.

"After listening to you question the patient, I feel you should have dug deeper in the history. You could have really missed something," he accused.

"Really? Well, Kyle, what would *you* have asked differently?"

"Well, uh, that's beside the point," he avoided.

"How so?" I challenged.

He quickly resumed his accusations, "Given the patient's history, I personally would have started him on antibiotics, regardless of whether they were necessary or not."

This was the *wrong* answer. I began to get irritated and defensive. I explained again to him the statistical evidence of diarrhea, the signs and symptoms of a bacterial infection and why it is wrong to use antibiotics so freely. I recognized the possibility of traveler's diarrhea (a short course of loose stools that affects people traveling internationally) which, again, is often self-limiting and unless the symptoms are severe, it is not necessary to prescribe antibiotics. I then pointed out that our people were experiencing a day or two of mild symptoms and then they were fine. This sparked a huge debate.

"You don't know anything about how we do things out here. We have to keep the boys in the fight, that's the goal," he strongly expressed.

"You know what Kyle, you're right, I don't know how things work out here, and I see your point of keeping them 'mission-ready,' so what is your regimen?"

"Well, it depends on the patient," he replied. Again...*wrong* answer.

"No....if you are going to treat someone with an antibiotic, you need to do it correctly." I was furious by this point. I was trying very hard not to lose my cool, but I could not believe the total lack of respect from him. As the discussion became heated, we decided to take it up to the roof to hash it out. We talked in circles and I realized he didn't want a solution as much as he wanted to get a rise out of me to see where I stood and what kind of a "threat" I would be to his "show." I had not anticipated this type of hostility from one the guys, but I imagined it would not be the last time Kyle and I would disagree. I knew I had to maintain my responsibility to practice safe medicine.

Surprisingly, once we finished arguing, we had a decent conversation and he explained the importance of their mission and specifically, the region we were in. He explained that because the people were so easily influenced the main fight was not on the battlefield but more in winning their hearts and minds despite all of the lies the Taliban tried to feed them. "Do you have any idea how difficult it is to turn an Islamic man against a fellow Islamic man?" he asked. I wondered if it was even possible. It was disheartening to see how much their religion - something the people held so sacred - was being used to manipulate them into doing unthinkable things. He then went on to explain the importance of the information we would be gathering by interacting with the people in the clinic.

I had to say that after our talk I did feel better, but I was still disappointed in how the first day of many at the firebase went, especially with how well I meshed with the other team I was with. I hoped it would get better; otherwise, it would be a long four months. They had

166 DAYS

a mission scheduled the next day. Due to our vulnerability with them gone, Becky and I would not be seeing patients in the clinic while they were out. Instead, we would man the radios in the OpCen. I said a prayer that night that nothing bad would happen, but I had a feeling deep in my gut something would.

CHAPTER **18**

Day 59
First Taste of War

27 June 2008

We woke up at 0330 to pull radio watch for the guys while they were out on their mission. It was expected to be relatively short, the team arriving back to the base early that afternoon. The team commander, Curtis, said he did not anticipate any contact, but cautioned the guys to be on the defensive as always when they traveled through hostile areas. They rolled out about 0430 and the day began.

I sat and watched as Becky gave me the rundown on how the radios worked and the standard operating procedures. I also learned how to operate the surveillance camera, which was quite impressive. I found myself somewhat overwhelmed with everything; having never seen or operated any of the equipment before, but Becky reassured me eventually it would become second nature. The morning was pretty quiet early on, filled with OJT on radios, conversations and the occasional Sudoku puzzle. Around 1030 the team got into their first firefight. The Taliban tried to ambush them and had placed a roadside IED along their route. Luckily the guys identified and destroyed it and engaged the enemy without injury. As the day went on, they got into several more fights and requested Close Air Support (CAS) several times for assistance in taking out the enemy.

During one encounter, a Rocket-propelled Grenade (RPG) took out an ANA vehicle and injured two of the soldiers inside. The report came over the radio: "We have one casualty with a gunshot wound (GSW) to the hand, and another with multiple GSWs to the chest."

"We should hear the 9-line medevac request soon," Becky said as we stood by the radio waiting anxiously for the next transmission. After a few minutes passed, it came.

"The patients have been stabilized, will maintain position and proceed to the firebase for medevac. Over," said the voice over the radio.

"That doesn't make any sense; didn't they say there was a casualty with multiple gunshot wounds to the chest?" I asked.

"I thought that's what he said," Becky answered. We looked back through our notes in confusion. The transmissions were intermittent and it was unclear what the status was with the patients, other than they were temporarily stabilized. For the next couple of hours, the team continued to engage the insurgents off and on. Becky and I sat on edge as we listened to their every word.

Along their route home they intercepted radio traffic from the enemy. We heard the radio operator's instructions come over: "Firebase, be advised, we anticipate enemy contact just east of the firebase, request for recon of this location with surveillance camera." We both ran to the camera and looked in the location they suspected, but we couldn't see any sign of activity.

I felt so helpless, imagining what they were going through; knowing somewhere, very close by, someone was waiting to attack them. We couldn't do anything but watch and wait. We watched with the camera as the trucks approached the gate, all of a sudden we heard a loud BOOM!! We scanned the footage on the camera and saw where an RPG impacted near the trucks. At that point the entire situation turned into chaos.

"Base! Get the medics out to the clinic to receive our casualties!" the voice screamed over the radio. Becky and I jumped up and grabbed our things and started to head out, all the while hearing

FIRST TASTE OF WAR

constant gunfire and RPG explosions right outside the gate of the firebase; and right by the clinic. As we hurried out the door, one of the guys who had stayed back with us came running after us.

"Becky! Stay here! I need you to man the radios. Jenn, go down to the clinic without her, I'm heading down to the mortar pit!"

What the??? I had no time to react, I just ran across the base as fast as I could, over the rocks, praying I wouldn't get hit as I heard the horrible booms and bangs of combat happening all around me. Once I got to the clinic, and inside the door, I ran to the trauma bays and made sure they were prepared to receive our casualties. I found myself running back and forth between the bays, frantically trying to prepare any and everything I might need, yet my emotions were so heightened, I couldn't think straight and found myself having to retrace my steps several times to make sure I didn't forget anything. And then....it happened. BOOM!!!

The explosion was so loud, and so close to the clinic, that it shook the entire building. In that instant; a moment that consisted of mere seconds, the most profound thing happened to me. I jumped off of the ground, with the most incredible fear I had ever experienced, and as soon as my feet hit the ground an unexplainable calm came over me. It was like someone flipped a switch in me that turned off all of the irrational thoughts provoked by fear, and turned my logic and common sense on. I remember telling myself, "Jenn, don't do this, not now. Get it together and do your job." That was all it took... I was in the zone. I can't begin to explain how it felt to go from feeling I could die, to being focused on the task at hand with such clarity; it seemed I had been doing this for years. The minutes seemed like hours, but I was ready to receive whatever came through the door.

Eventually the booms stopped, but were quickly replaced with the banging on the door to the back entrance to the clinic. As I walked to the door I replayed everything I learned in my training about inserting a chest tube and controlling bleeding from blast injuries and gunshot wounds. I was ready for whatever was behind the door - or so I thought.

Expecting to see our guys when I opened the door, I was shocked to find a truck filled with local nationals who had been escorted in by the ANA. In the backseat I saw a child lying in his blood soaked clothes with his father beside him, screaming frantically at me in Pashtu to help his child. I found myself unprepared and completely caught off guard for this situation. *Where were our guys? Were they a triage priority over this little boy? Where was a Terp to help me understand what they were screaming at me?* I was expecting multiple gunshot wounds to the chest and a hand wound! I stumbled through my thoughts and I looked to my right and saw the HMMWVs and Kyle (my most recently acquired nemesis) standing outside. I waved him over to get some clarity.

"Where are our casualties?" I yelled.

"They haven't made it to the base yet."

"What about the patient with the chest wounds? Is he still stable?"

He looked at me with confused eyes and said, "What are you talking about? We don't have anyone shot in the chest. We have a leg wound and a hand wound." I felt instant relief despite my confusion.

"Help me carry this boy into the clinic so we can assess his wounds," I said. Despite our previous confrontation he quickly ran over to assist. Becky quickly joined us and together we got the boy inside. Once he was on the table, I cut away his clothes and was able to see the extent of his injuries. He had a wound in his right upper abdomen from an RPG that was deep enough that it exposed part of his liver and bowel. The entire left side of his abdomen was rigid and distended leaving me to believe he had significant internal bleeding. Thankfully all of my emergency room experience surfaced and we stabilized him in textbook order. It was quite a sight to see. Becky, Kyle and I; three strangers just days ago, now working in harmony as a team to try to save this boy.

"Becky, I need you to control any external bleeding, get IV access and wait for my order for medications," I instructed.

"I'm all over it," she answered.

"Kyle, elevate his feet. Let's try to keep him warm; we don't need him going into shock or developing hypothermia."

"No problem," he replied, "I'm also keeping a log of vital signs every five minutes and will let you know if there is any change."

"Great, thanks." I said. "Becky we need to give him a fluid bolus, but it needs to be calculated on his weight."

"Alright, I'll get it ready," she quickly answered and ran to the pharmacy to get the fluids. Hal came in and began to take down the necessary information for the 9-line medevac to get the boy back to the surgeons I had just left at TK.

"Just so you guys are aware, the two ANA patients are stable and ready for medevac," Hal said.

"Ok, it was a hand and leg wound?" I asked. I looked up as I prepared the medications for the boy.

"Yes ma'am, all superficial, the bleeding is controlled and dressings applied," he said.

"Nice work Hal." I said.

It was interesting to watch Kyle in this situation. Mr. "Know it All" from the day before completely backed off and watched me run the show. As time passed, I became increasingly concerned for the boy due to the extent of his wounds and the high risk for infection, given the nature of his injuries. I could see his bowel was clearly perforated, which meant he now had feces in his abdominal cavity and the potential for him to decompensate quickly was very real - whether it be from respiratory distress or hypovolemia (low blood volume). I knew if we didn't get him out soon we would be in a situation none of us wanted to be in. We managed to keep him stable and comfortable for the next hour until the medevac helicopter landed. Once the helicopter arrived we loaded him, and the two stable ANA casualties on board and it was over.

After cleaning the blood off of the equipment, putting the clinic back together, and prepping to receive whatever else was out there, we went up to the OpCen for the After Actions briefing. We sat and listened to the details of the mission and report of the estimate of the enemies killed in action (KIAs) being in the thirties. As I looked around the room at these men, I sensed relief that it was over, but the hunger for another fight was behind each of their eyes. I couldn't begin to comprehend the mentality it took to be able to do what they did every day.

When the meeting was over, I got up quietly, walked to my room with Becky following close behind, both of us knowing what would happen next. We closed the door and collapsed in each other's arms and I finally cried.

CHAPTER **19**

Day 62
Settling In

30 June 2008

The last couple of days consisted of a lot of administrative work with the clinic. We got the patient bays organized and the pharmacy in order. The pharmacy was almost completely stocked with expired medications, so I had to completely re-inventory and organize it. Becky, the other medics and I did some brainstorming and came up with an idea to provide classes on basic medical knowledge for the general population as well as the women, specifically for female-related healthcare issues. We also decided to come up with some radio broadcasts consisting of medical advice and tips on prevention of the most common ailments for the population, such as diarrhea and dehydration. I was pleased with our ideas and was relieved we could come together as a team. Becky also had a good idea about putting a "comment box" of sorts in the clinic for the patients to put their questions and/or any information they wished to relay to us in. I hoped the ideas would be fruitful and not just talk, as so many ideas often were.

We had several team meetings as well, all of which consisted of the same theme - fighting. Over the next month it was expected there would be a lot of fighting, since it was the prime season for the Taliban, which meant I would be seeing very few "routine" clinic cases, and focusing more on the traumas from the missions. After each of these meetings, the guys picked up and shipped out for another mission. I got so nervous every time they went out. The Taliban wanted their firebase back, and I hated being in such a vulnerable position.

After one of the first meetings, Becky and I went to our room, and shortly after Hal came running in. "Guys! We're getting attacked! Get your gear on and get to the OpCen as soon as possible!" We rushed to get our flak vests, helmets, and weapons on as quickly as possible and ran to where we were instructed to meet. As we arrived in a state of panic we saw no one was there.

"What's going on?" Becky asked. Suddenly we heard laughter.

"Come on," I said. We slowly made our way back to our room. As we walked outside we heard a large eruption of laughter above us. We looked up and saw the majority of the team on the roof laughing and pointing at us. It was all a joke. The guys thought it would be funny to see us run out of our room as fast as we could in our full gear, so they sent Hal in to deliver the instructions while the rest of them waited for the show.

"Sorry guys! We had to do it! Man you should have seen your faces!" Hal laughed.

"Ha ha! Very funny!" Becky said, as we went back to our room. Initially I was hurt we were the butt of their joke, but then I realized it was their way of keeping things light, and they would have done it to anyone. I was able to see the humor in it, but I couldn't disregard the real threat that was out there, and the potential violence that could occur. I felt very insecure about what my role would be if things did get bad. I didn't want to engage in contact, but the reality of the situation was I might have to. Through the deployment I tried hard to stay healthy; mentally and physically, but it was not easy. Already I could see my mental well-being wavering and slipping at times. I talked with Greg about it and he agreed the journal was the best avenue for me to channel my feelings.

CHAPTER **20**

Day 63
Casualties of War

1 July 2008

It was a day filled with nothing but badness all around. It started with Becky getting very sick in the middle of the night with another episode of gastroenteritis; vomiting and suffering from diarrhea all night. I woke up several times trying to help by giving her what medications I could, but she still suffered the whole night and into the day with her symptoms.

Clinic that day seemed to go the way Becky felt. The day before I'd seen a little five-year-old boy who fell approximately eight feet off of his roof. When I initially saw him he was fine, only complaining of shoulder pain, but responsive and smiling. If this were a patient I were seeing back home, I would have been able to get a head CAT Scan to fully evaluate if there was a severe head injury, but I only had his father's words to go by and what I could see on physical exam.

"IG, tell the dad I am going to tell him what he needs to look for in his son over the next twenty four hours," I instructed my Terp. As IG told the man what I asked him, the man nodded eagerly as he helplessly waited for instructions to help his son. "You need to watch him overnight and if he stops eating, starts sleeping all the time, or if he throws up more than four times I need you to bring him back to me,"

I said. The father agreed and took his son home.

Sure enough he was back the very next day. The boy had completely changed in just one day; all of the things I told his father to watch for had happened. During the physical exam I saw something alarming that was not present the day before. In the medical world we call it "Battle's Signs," which is bruising behind the ear, a finding that is consistent with a basilar skull fracture. I examined the affected side of his head and discovered the entire left side was swollen and when I pushed I could feel the edema - another sign of a serious injury to his head.

"Sir, I am so sorry, but your son's injuries are severe, and I have limited capabilities here in this clinic. I can only treat his symptoms." The man began to cry. "If you can get him to TK or Kandahar there are much larger facilities to treat his condition."

He looked at me with tear-filled eyes and began to speak. Through IG he said, "I have already walked for several hours to get to you. I have no money or means of transportation to get my son to those places." I could feel my own eyes filling with tears. He went on, "Even if I did walk to TK, the Taliban would surely kill me or my son."

"Why would they kill you for traveling to TK?" I asked.

"They know I would be traveling there for the help of the infidels," he answered. I tried to fathom what it must be like to be in his shoes and I couldn't comprehend it.

"IG, tell him to wait here, I will go and see if there is a way I can arrange for transportation for him." I tried everything I could to help him, but I was unsuccessful. "Sir, I am so sorry, I have no way to get you there," I explained.

"I know. It is what it is," he said. I could see he had given up. I gave the boy a steroid shot, hoping to decrease the swelling and inflammation. I packed up some medicine for pain and the nausea and handed it to the boy's father.

"We can continue to monitor the boy if you would like to bring him back, there's a chance he could pull through this injury," I said, as I handed the medications to the man. I knew as I spoke the words it was likely not the truth; given the environment had none of the necessary medical care available, coupled with his rapid deterioration, his outlook was dismal at best.

The man took the bags I gave him and put his hand over his heart and nodded to me. He picked up his child, turned and walked away. As he left I felt his genuine gratitude for the care we were able to provide, which made it that much harder to watch him walk away carrying his son into the abyss of Afghanistan, never to be seen by me again.

After I completed my day in the clinic, I went back to the room to check on Becky. She was sleeping finally, so I decided to check my email. While I was logged on I decided to email Don and Chad, I was thinking about how the mission they went on after we did the MedCap together. I knew they had a long week and were likely just getting back. Shortly after I sent the email I heard back from Don. I read his words in complete disbelief:

Jenn,
I just got back to the firebase and others are due here tonight. I do not know if you have heard the jacked up news; however, here it goes. We were on the combat patrol and after no sleep for over 30 hours we decided to RON [remain overnight]. When we started to get things ready to RON Travis stepped on a mine and was killed. I kept him alive for 30 minutes; however, both arms and from the pelvis down was missing. I cut him open and crossed clamped his aorta, however, he died shortly after that. I would say that out of the 27 years I have treated trauma cases, this was the most devastating. Both arms and just at the waist-line were gone. I did what I could and I am glad that Travis lived until the medevac came. I feel really bad that he died; I really tried everything and thought that he would live despite the wounds. I flew back with all four individuals to TK FST. After his death I escorted him to KAF. I still have a hard time with it. I was just done talking

> to Travis and was going to walk with him up front, but I went toward my truck instead and that is when he stepped on the mine. I am glad that I was there to work on Travis and direct the medics. If I was not there, I think that they all would have died because it was overwhelming for the team medics to see Travis like that and they would have been working on Travis and would not have been able to focus on the others. From the start of this mission, everyone had a bad feeling. The first night we had my truck break down and would not start. We finally got it started and Matt's truck broke down. My truck had to tow Matt's. We were about to head to the pass when the second truck broke. If we had gone through that night, I sincerely believe that we would have had many from the team dead. Three others were injured.

I remembered hearing chatter on the radio that a US Special Forces troop was killed a couple of days prior to the email, but I never heard who it was and I never thought it would be a friend. As I read the words on the screen I began to cry. Not Travis! Out of all the guys I met on that team, he was by far one of my favorites. He was only twenty-four years old. He had a wife and a great sense of humor.

Don explained in the email that three other ANA and interpreters were injured as well, but they survived and were sent to BAF for definitive care. One lost a finger and one had over thirty fractures to his face. To make matters even worse, the next day the Battalion sent a team to retrieve Travis's extremities and they got their vehicle, an, RG-33, stuck in a creek and three of them drowned.

I cried and cried. I felt sick to my stomach. I couldn't get Travis out of my head; I kept seeing his shit-eating grin and joyful eyes. Why did this happen? What is the purpose of losing such a great person? Or losing the three soldiers who went back to collect his remains?

I remembered again the last time I saw him while I was waiting for my flight out at TK; I gave him a hug and heard his haunting words, "We do it because we love it; don't worry about us." Now he was gone. I was aware that soldiers were dying every day, but naively I never expected to be so personally affected. I, like many others, had developed a false sense of distance from the inevitable loss that comes with war. Sadly, I now had a new understanding of the reality of wartime.

Day 66
Independence Day

4 July 2008

I have to say without a doubt that this 4th of July has been the most significant one in my life. For the past twenty-seven years I enjoyed the family barbeques, fireworks and friends in the comfort and relative safety of the borders of the United States. I had no concept of the true meaning of this holiday. I had never made a sacrifice for my country and never known anyone who had given their life for it. Of course, like any red-blooded American, I celebrated it with pride, but the sacrifice behind what made the day possible was always something I read about in books, not anything that was personal. Now, I had lost a friend to this horrible war, been on a firebase that had been attacked by enemy fire, seen the poverty and the toll hundreds of years of war had taken on the country of Afghanistan and its people, and I was looking at this holiday through a new set of eyes ...eyes of understanding and true appreciation.

I looked out at the mountainous horizons of Afghanistan, saddened to know now firsthand there are people in this world who have no idea what it means to have freedom or experience its benefits as we Americans have. Even more saddening was the realization that Americans, including myself, had such a horrible habit of taking what we had in our nation for granted; having no concept of what it is like to live without the luxuries we have come to *expect* as a right, not something we have earned. I openly admit to being just as guilty of this. It sickened me that I, like so many Americans, had *no* idea what was happening in the country of Afghanistan prior to my deployment. It saddened me that the American youth was growing up in a generation of tablets, cell phones, and fancy cars, completely missing the bigger picture of what was happening in the world outside of our "American Bubble".

Unfortunately, I spent the majority of the day in bed, sick with diarrhea....perhaps Kyle would recommend an antibiotic for me. In the evening we had a barbeque to acknowledge our country and what we were all there for and I managed to drag myself out of bed to attend. I sat outside on a bench, and in between my trips to the bathroom, I looked at the guys that surrounded me and I had an overwhelming sense of pride to be sharing this day with them. I looked at them all and smiled, listening to them laugh and give each other a hard time. I glanced up at the roof of the OpCen at our beautiful American flag flying with honor and pride even though she was flying at half-mast to pay tribute to an American soldier who, just days before, had made the ultimate sacrifice like many before him and many after him would continue to make.

I decided to go up to the roof to be alone with my thoughts. As I sat there, as the sun was setting over Afghanistan, I couldn't take my eyes off the flag flying at half-mast for my friend. I sat alone, letting the tears of grief stream down my face; grateful to have known a brave soldier like Travis who proudly served knowing of the dangers he faced… and loving every minute of it.

CHAPTER **21**

Day 67
Another Year Older

5 July 2008

Even though I turned twenty-eight on this day, it didn't feel like a birthday. We hadn't been able to receive mail in several weeks, so I had no cards or presents to open from my friends and family. It was just another day in Afghanistan, but people did try to make it seem special. Greg was so sweet and sent me an email video of him singing me "Happy Birthday". I watched it over and over, watching his silly attempt to make me smile.

My mom, my sister Karri, and her kids threw me a birthday party and sent pictures over email. I tried to call them but was unable to get through. I did speak to Greg's parents and little Griffen, my stepson. It was so hard to talk to Griff; as soon as he heard my voice his got very quiet and I could hear him holding back tears. He was so sad, which in turn made me even more upset to be away from my loved ones. I missed everyone so much.

As I sat in my room missing my family terribly, I heard a knock. "Hey guys, we have a little party with music, come on!" Manuel said. He was the communications sergeant on the team and was lighthearted and fun to be around. His jokes were horrible, but they always made us laugh and I could use a good laugh.

ANOTHER YEAR OLDER

"Come on Jenn! It's your birthday!" Becky pleaded.

"Your birthday? See! I knew we should have a party!" Manuel laughed. "Tell you what; I will put on my special 'Danger' cologne for the occasion." Becky and I burst into laughter; he had taken the cologne from one of the enemy compounds they had raided in the last several days. He came back to the firebase yelling *"Danger!"* each time he sprayed it. Its name suited it well; it was probably the most horrible cologne I had ever smelled. It had become a running joke with him; he carried it with him everywhere, spraying it as often as he could.

"Danger!" Becky and I said in unison.

"Alright, let's go," I said and we went to the party. Manuel brought ponchos from home that he handed out to everyone and we took turns wearing his sombrero. We all sat around the table in our ponchos listening to music and laughing, and for a few short moments we disappeared in our fellowship and the sadness we had all been feeling faded away.

After the party was over, I went up to the roof of the OpCen for a few moments alone. As I watched the sun setting over the mountains, I wondered what my twenty-eighth year would bring. How could I live my life better than I had last year? What did I learn? What would I take with me from this experience to better myself? I'd grown up so much as a person in the last two years, let alone the last two months. I was grateful for the path God had chosen for me and the lessons I'd learned by the experiences I'd encountered. As I sat there alone in my thoughts, 7,000 miles away from everything and everyone I knew and loved, I was thankful for where I was and doing the things I was doing. I knew these six months of my life would undoubtedly be six months that would impact me for a lifetime. It had made my heart and soul open to so much more. I missed everyone back home so much it hurt, yet I knew I was exactly where I needed to be, and I couldn't wait to see what the next year had in store.

CHAPTER **22**

Day 72
Touching Hands

10 July 2008

There was a supply drop scheduled just outside the gate of the firebase which required the team to go out in the vehicles, set up a security perimeter, collect the supplies, and bring them back to the firebase. On this particular drop Curtis, the team commander, decided while they were out he wanted to do a "Mini MedCap" in the village next to the Drop Zone.

It was a well-received idea by everyone involved. The team wanted to spread the word to the local people that Becky and I were there and we were eager to meet more of them, specifically the women and children. We also wanted to inform the women of the educational classes we were hoping to start.

Once the perimeter was secured, and we had all of our gear and weapons on, we headed out on the ATVs into the area just outside the "safety" of our firebase walls. As soon as we got to the Drop Zone we saw children running up as fast as they could to greet us. One little girl walked up to both Becky and me and grabbed our hands, rubbed our skin with a look of disbelief on her face, as if she were checking to see if we were really standing there in front of her.

Curtis watched her reaction to us and smiled saying, "Look! She is rubbing your hands because she can't believe you are real!" I will never forget the smile on her face that extended from ear to ear when she realized two *American Women* were in fact very real and standing right in front of her!

"You see my sisters, this 'American woman' is a figure these girls only talked about, but have never seen in this area of the country," said Hanifi, one of the Terps, explained.

"Wow...that's incredible," Becky said.

"You must realize, seeing you is something very special to these little girls, they never forget," he explained. I was honored, I had been completely oblivious to the impact we had until that moment.

The other children swarmed around us shortly thereafter, eyes filled with wonderment and smiles of gratitude. We handed out cookies and candy for a few minutes and after the excitement wore down Curtis asked, "Are you ready to meet with the village elders?"

"Yeah, of course," I replied "where do we go?"

"Our plan is to meet with them inside the compound...standby and let me see what's going on," He said as he went with a Terp into the compound to see if the men were ready.

"Can you believe this?" Becky asked as the children played with our sunglasses and helmets. One little girl walked around wearing my sunglasses on her head as she had seen me wearing them earlier. She was fascinated with me and wouldn't leave my side. As I sat she played with my hair just like any little girl would back home.

"It's amazing," I answered. "I wish we could give them so much more than what we have with us."

"Me too," Becky agreed.

We handed the kids backpacks filled with school supplies, Band-Aids, lotion, and hygiene kits. We taught them how to brush their teeth and put lotion on their dry skin. As I taught them how to use the toothbrush I looked into their mouths, and was shocked to see what horrible condition their teeth were in. They did not have access to toothpaste and toothbrushes; such a simple thing in America. We gave out multi-vitamins and blew up exam gloves and drew on faces magically transforming them into fun balloons to play with. The little girls followed us everywhere we walked, holding our hands, and rubbing the lotion that we had just given to them on our hands. They even offered me a piece of the candy that just minutes before they had fought over with all their might. We were lost in the moment with them, hearing their laughter and seeing their smiles warmed my heart. I looked up and saw Curtis walking towards us.

"Becks," I said using my nickname for Becky, "Here comes Curtis. It must be time for us to meet the village elders."

"I'm excited to see the inside of the compound," Becky said. I remembered the compound I had seen in my first MedCap. We stood and began to gather our things.

"Well, change of plans, we are going to meet with the elders right here," Curtis said.

"Why? I thought we were going into the compound?" Becky asked.

"Well, apparently that's not a possibility," he answered.

I wondered if it had anything to do with the fact that we were women, but we would never know. Regardless, as we talked to the elders, they expressed sincere gratitude to us for taking care of their families and they were elated we were there. We exchanged our thanks for their support of the Coalition Forces.

"They would like to sit and drink chai with you," Hanifi said. "This is a big honor."

"Of course, we would love to," I said and we sat together. They thanked us again and again for being there and suddenly the eldest elder stood up and began to speak.

"He wants to offer thanks with a feast," Hanifi translated.

"Well, that is very generous of him, please thank him, but I believe we are going to be leaving soon," I said as I looked at Curtis to confirm.

"Oh no Miss Jennifer, he give you a chicken," he explained.

"Oh...um...wow...that's...uh," I stumbled over my words.

"This is probably one of his family's most valuable possessions, giving it to you is a huge deal," Curtis added.

"I am honored," I replied, as I truly was. It was an incredible gesture. The elder returned with a very small white chicken, legs tied together with a string and handed it to me. I put my hand over my heart and nodded in thanks as I accepted the chicken. I pictured my husband standing there watching me and laughing as I held the chicken; he knew the *last* thing I would do is kill that bird and eat it; instead, it would become a pet or a camp mascot. I could just imagine if I were home and having to deal with Greg and my new pet chicken running around in the backyard. It made me smile.

It turned into a very awkward moment for me, because instead of accepting the gift and getting on the ATVs and leaving, I ended up standing there with the bird for about thirty minutes waiting for team to get ready to go. The team guys got a good laugh out of watching me stand there with my chicken, trying not to let it wiggle out of my hands or poop on my clothes. I must admit, it was a pretty funny sight, but I was deeply moved by the gesture, especially being a woman in a country with a culture that typically holds women in such a low regard.

It was soon time to say goodbye. We packed up our things and said our farewells. I hated to leave; the children had found so much joy in the little time that we spent with them. As I watched them stare at Becky and me with joy and amazement, I realized how such small gestures and the simplest things meant so much. I began to think of my own childhood and how poor I thought we were because we could never afford family vacations or fancy things like all of my friends. But as I watched these children play with our balloons, made out of exam gloves, I realized how blessed I really was. I always had toys and a warm home with shoes to cover my feet and clothes to keep me dry. I never truly *needed* for anything, and as I reminisced, I felt ashamed for constantly wanting more than I had.

As we rode off on the ATVs I waved one last time. Even though we were the ones who came bearing gifts, I felt I left with the most valuable gift of the day; a peek inside their world; which in turn, made me appreciate my own so much more.

Day 76
Similarities across Oceans

14 July 2008

We began to notice a new trend in the patient load. Our days were becoming significantly busier and we were seeing many more women and children. When I first arrived, we were seeing one-to-two a morning, but we had now transitioned into spending the majority of our time with the women. It was nice to see the word of our presence was spreading in a positive light.

I saw one lady in particular with a burn on her arm who came with a friend I had seen the day before. As I was treating the lady's burn, I watched her talk with her friend and shyly looking back at me giggling. I knew they were talking about me and smiled. Soon I figured out what they were talking about. Her friend pointed to my face and to the patient's face where she had several freckles. I too had many freckles in the same place on my face. She then pointed to her friend's nose ring and pointed to my ears to show that we also both had piercings. What a neat moment in time I had shared with these ladies. Despite all of the differences in our cultures and individual lives and hardships, we still had similarities. We all three had a tender laugh together as I finished treating her burn. I wondered to myself how she could have gotten such a burn. Unfortunately the most likely source was her "loving" husband. What a different world. As the ladies got up to leave they both hugged me and kissed my cheeks expressing sincere thanks. They covered their hearts with their hands and said "Tashikor" which was "Thank you" in Dari. As I watched them leave, I told myself it was moments like this one that I would treasure for the rest of my life.

Before clinic I had heard news of a suicide bombing at a bazaar the day before that killed over thirty locals. As I inquired more about where this occurred, I discovered it was in the exact location I had performed the first MedCap. I actually received an email from Chad (the medic from the first MedCap) about the incident. He told me that they took care of many of the victims, some of whom did not survive.

My stomach turned. Instant flashbacks of the angry faces of the men in black walking behind our vehicles in the convoy surfaced in my head. It was sobering to think that the area of the attack was not far at all from where our firebase was located. I would never be able to fathom the extent of violence in this country. The children never had a childhood and the women lived in constant fear while the men knew nothing else but a life of fighting…whether it was defending their families and farms from the Taliban, or from us.

I tried to put these thoughts out of my head and continue with clinic patients. After about an hour the team sergeant came down and said, "Time to close up shop here guys, we are going out on a mission."

"Alright, we just need to get the last few patients out," I answered. I finished handing the medications I prescribed to my last patient, and as I walked her out I looked up and watched our "trusted" gate guards let three people walk into the clinic without searching them. As I stated before, the clinic was right on the edge of the firebase and the only thing separating us from *them* was some C-wire and these guards who were instructed to search every patient and scan them with a metal detector wand. The women were often in burkas, which covered them from head-to-toe, the only opening was a mesh-type area over the eyes for them to see out of. We had been informed the Taliban had used this to their advantage and developed a tactic of wearing burkas with a bomb strapped to their chests knowing no one would touch them. Additionally, the Taliban were also known to have bombs folded up in their turbans or in their robes.

We all looked in shock as we watched the people walk through the gate and up to the clinic. How many times had this happened that we didn't know of? Talk about a false sense of security!

"Are you kidding me?!" Becky yelled.

"Don't worry, I'll take care of this," Kyle said and headed over to the guards. We watched him as he firmly reminded the men about the threat and importance of their jobs in defending the clinic and the firebase. They appeared to listen intently, scrambling to find the metal detectors they weren't using.

"I can't believe this! We're trusting these incompetent guards with our safety. I don't even want to think about how many people we have seen that could've easily come into the clinic with weapons or suicide bombs," I said.

"My God, I know-seeing this the day after that bombing makes me feel sick to my stomach," Becky added.

"Me too," I said. I could feel an intense nausea consuming me, it became more than I could handle. Ben, the team guy responsible for the guards, had made his way down to the clinic and saw how upset we were.

"What happened?" he asked.

"Ben, these guards aren't checking the people that come through for anything! They are just letting them walk right up to the clinic. We are a huge target, which already makes us feel uneasy. And now we just witnessed firsthand their complete disregard for security the day after a significant bombing in the same province."

"Oh hell no! I'll be right back," Ben said as he ran down to the guard post and got in the face of the head guard and echoed the same message Kyle had just delivered. The men quickly nodded their heads in understanding as Ben continued to light them up. After several more minutes the guys returned to the clinic.

"That won't happen again," Ben reassured.

"I hope not, thank you," I said uneasily, hoping it made a difference.

"Are you guys ok to close up? We have to get back up to the OpCen to load up for the mission," asked Ben.

"Yeah, we'll be fine. See you up there," I answered and they left. Becky and I sat alone in silence in our clinic. "All we can do is be

SIMILARITIES ACROSS OCEANS

more vigilant about monitoring what's coming through the gate."

"I pray that's enough," Becky said. I did too…

After we closed the clinic, we came back up to the OpCen and helped the team prepare and depart for their mission. As I assisted the guys with gear and water, I realized the longer I was there, the more I understood what was going on in the different locations and tribes; the area we were in had an unbelievable Taliban influence. My mind returned to the clinic and what a vulnerable target we were.

The mission kept the team out late into the evening. When they returned we all sat and had the After Action briefing and were then dismissed to retire to bed. After the meeting, I found myself sitting outside under a full moon and sky full of stars talking with Curtis about what they had accomplished during their mission and since their arrival in the area. He talked specifically about one family he had encountered.

"I could tell as soon as I began talking to them, it was evident they had been deeply brainwashed by the propaganda of the Taliban. The more I talked with the father, and showed respect, the more the man opened up. By the end of the conversation, he was showing us both support and appreciation."

"Wow, that's incredible."

"Yeah, it was. He told me he'd never seen Americans before, and he touched my face and hands….then he said everything that he had been told about us was wrong."

"How interesting that one conversation, one encounter, could change so much," I said. Curtis went on to tell me the progress of the Coalition Forces had made in establishing a local government despite tribal differences. He explained that the mere idea of these people working together was completely out of reach just a few years earlier, and now it was happening right before our eyes. What an amazing thing to witness. Maybe, just maybe, we had many more similarities than just freckles and piercings.

Medevac for Manuel

US Army Photos

Hal calling OpCen over radio

Village elder giving Jenn a chicken

Little girl touching Jenn's hand because she didn't believe she was real

Jenn & Becky at clinic next to a picture a child sent to them from the US

Little girl wearing Jenn's helmet

Rod & Jacko at the firebase

Jenn paying tribute to Rod at his memorial on the firebase

Jenn visiting Rod's grave in 2012

Jenn standing with the firebase behind her

CHAPTER **23**

Day 77
Missing My Gerg

15 July 2008

This entry is nothing more, and nothing less, than my sincere longing to be with my husband and best friend. I missed him so much, more and more as each day passed. I thought of him constantly and longed to be with him and in the safety of his arms. These feelings continued to intensify as I read his emails and heard his voice on the phone. I knew during our time apart, he too was going through a personal journey of his own. This time would continue to make us resilient as we both grew individually. We would both come out of this experience as stronger people and an even stronger "us". I couldn't begin to imagine the heartache and sense of helplessness he must have been feeling, knowing very little about what I was doing and the dangers I faced. I couldn't tell him the majority of what was happening, nor did I want to. I couldn't stand to think of him worrying about me any more than he already was. It would be awful to hear your wife was in a location that was under attack on a regular basis and there was little-to-no security around where she was every day.

It had become the norm to expect some sort of small arms fire, mortar attempts, or even RPGs on a regular basis. It had initially been a very scary thing for both Becky and me; however, as time went on we became used to it, something I would've never thought possible before this deployment. No…Greg didn't need to know that. I loved him with all of my heart and soul and wanted him to get through our time apart as painlessly as possible.

CHAPTER **24**

Days 80-86
Divine Intervention

18-24 July 2008

Occasionally, visitors arrived at the firebase on the ring flight with our mail and supplies. Sometimes they were in transit to other locations, and sometimes they were sent to our firebase specifically. They stayed until the next flight out, which was most often a week. On this particular ring flight we received a special kind of visitor, an Army Chaplin. He was traveling around to various locations to bring ministry, prayers, and comfort to the troops in the forward locations in the best ways he could. This was an amazing gift, especially considering how remote we were and the types of circumstances we faced every single day. I hoped it would be a way to lift our morale and reinforce the spirituality that is often forgotten with the nature of the business.

He was very friendly, and surprisingly, had an appreciation and respect for the team and what their mission was. I was impressed to hear he'd actually completed the qualification course (Q-Course) the Green Berets go through. While he felt war was an awful reality, it was just that, a reality that was happening, and he wanted to continue to focus on the grace and human element within the soldiers fighting to help them find peace in what they had to do. He spent a lot of time with Becky and me in the OpCen while the team was out, but he made an effort to seek out individuals on the team as well, often ministering to them one-on-one as they allowed.

He asked if we could have a service one night, and only those who wanted to attend were asked to be present. We sat on the roof on a beautiful evening as the sun was setting in the horizon. There were a handful of us in attendance, I had hoped for more. Becky, Hal, and I felt it was a service that was absolutely needed, and we happily accepted the invitation. He handed us each a copy of the New Testament and we prayed. We prayed for strength to deal with the harsh realities of war and to move on from it once we left this place. He had a beautiful sermon about finding the good in the unfortunate situation that occurred frequently during this and perhaps other deployments. It was perfectly appropriate for our circumstances, and where I felt I was on a personal spiritual level.

As I listened to him speak, I couldn't help but notice he was standing in front of the M240 machine gun that was used to defend the firebase as we were so frequently attacked. What irony. I never would have imagined I would be listening to a sermon such as this in such a hostile place with horribly violent and inhuman acts happening all around me, but I was. When he concluded, he asked us to join and sing several hymns. It was an awkward silence initially. The only voice that we heard was the Chaplin's. Asking these men, who were so hardened from their duties, to sing together, with no music was not the most comfortable thing for them to do. Eventually, more and more of them began to sing, and I felt I was witnessing a very rare instance, seeing these fighters let their guard down and be vulnerable; it was a moment I would never forget.

The Chaplin's time with us came to a quick end, I hated that he was leaving; I felt that his presence helped me understand why we were there. I think we all took our own personal meaning from the time we shared with him, but I knew I needed that spiritual reminder that our God was still present despite the ugliness of the world we were witnessing on an everyday basis.

CHAPTER 25

Days 87-88
Close Encounters of the Taliban Kind

25 July 2008

My hands are literally shaking as I write this. The guys were going out on a mission, as scheduled, early in the morning and, as usual, Becky and I helped them get loaded up on the vehicles and took our positions manning the radios. While each vehicle had a person operating our radios, several also had an interpreter monitoring the channels the Taliban were known to use. It was helpful to the missions to listen in on what the enemy plans were. As the convoy of vehicles left the base, we settled in for what we thought would be a very long day. I pulled out my Sudoku puzzle and medical journal and propped my feet up on the table.

Two minutes after leaving the gate, Curtis came over the radio stating the mission was compromised and they were returning to the base. Becky and I looked at each other in confusion.

"What do you think that's about?" Becky asked.

"I honestly have no clue," I said. As they pulled in front of the OpCen several of the guys kept their armor and weapons on and proceeded to walk up to the ANA camp on the firebase. Our friend Roy made his way into the OpCen and saw the confusion on our faces.

"The Captain had strong reason to believe, after several failed missions, there's a leak to the Taliban from someone in the ANA," he explained.

"Are you kidding me?" I said.

"Nope, and as time has gone on he developed even more reason to believe that the *someone* was not just anyone, but the ANA Commander himself." Becky and I were speechless. He continued, "So Curtis purposely told him, and only him, false information about the details of the mission hoping to catch him in the act. Sure enough, as we were leaving the interpreters heard the information that was passed on to the Commander being discussed between the Taliban voices on the other end of the radio."

As I listened to Roy I was stunned and mortified at the same time. I had been left alone countless of times with this man on the firebase. How easily things could have gone badly. As I thought about it, I recalled several previous missions he did not participate in because he didn't "feel well," prompting a visit to the clinic. Ironically, those same missions ended up with some significant firefights and very close calls. Becky and I rushed over to the security camera and watched in horror as five team guys, and some of the ANA soldiers, drew their rifles on the Commander outside of his room. We, and everyone else on the firebase, were anticipating a huge rebellion from the ANA soldiers and a very bad situation with a stand-off between us and them.

I watched him on the camera as the whole thing happened. I could see it in his face, even before they got to his camp, that he knew he was caught. I watched him sit on a table and smoke a cigarette, trying to appear as if nothing was wrong, calm as could be, but we all knew better. He knew it was over, in more ways than one. After what seemed like hours of watching them talk to him, they finally took the traitor into custody and kept him in holding until he could be escorted off of the firebase and out of our lives.

Several days later he was loaded on the helicopter that came in as a ring flight, and I felt an unnerving sense of relief, relief that he was no longer in the same location, but unnerving because it made me question from that moment on who else of those with us was one of *them*. The phrase, "sleep with one eye open" had never been more personal, real, and true.

26 July 2008

It was supposed to start just like any other clinic day; the doors opened at 0900 and closed at 1200 with plans to fill the afternoon with whatever tasks would arise. As I was getting dressed, and getting my gear together, I heard a knock on my door.

"Jenn, we need you down at the clinic, there's an emergency patient who's unconscious!" Roy yelled.

"Ok, I'm coming!" I grabbed my things and ran to the clinic as fast as I could. I entered through the back door as I always did and hurried to unlock the front door, which opened into an area only feet away from the border of the firebase. I saw the gate guards and someone lying underneath a blanket with two men squatted beside him just outside the C-wire of the base. I walked up to the guards with Roy and my Terp. "Hanifi, ask them if they have searched these men," I demanded.

"They say no Miss Jennifer," he answered.

"Well, you tell them I am not treating *anyone* until they're properly searched; emergency or not. That patient isn't coming to me and I'm not going to him until proper procedures are followed!" I insisted. My jaw was clenched and my heart pounding in anger at their continued disregard for my safety. I looked back at the clinic and saw Becky coming towards me.

"Jenn! What the hell does he have?" she asked. She pointed at one of the men beside the man under the blanket who had a shiny object in his hand and was holding it up to his ear. We assumed this was a cell phone. Something that was second nature to Americans was quite an uncommon luxury in this region of Afghanistan.

"Tell the guards to clear out the rest of the people waiting to be seen in clinic now and search these men! Do it now!" I screamed. Almost instantly the guards drew their AK-47s and begin to search the men. This sent chills down my spine as I recalled the recent suicide bombing. Becky and I backed up out of the way and continued to watch as the guards and our guys searched for the shiny object. After several minutes, they came up empty; the object had "mysteriously" disappeared. Our unease was palpable. All of a sudden the unconscious man who was our "emergency" woke up. After the search was complete, and the men were cleared, they were brought up to the clinic.

We noticed these men looked significantly different than the normal people we saw every day at the clinic. Our patient had a long beard and shaved head, which was often a sign of authority. The men with him were dressed in shorter, better kept tunics than the locals.

"Becky, don't touch them yet, stay with the Terps, I'm going to get Kyle and Hal." I ran up to the OpCen and banged on Hal's door. "You need to get down to the clinic right now. We have a sketchy situation," I said, and explained the details of what had happened.

"I'll get Kyle and we'll be right there," Hal said calmly. I was reassured by this, but at the same time frustrated because he didn't seem to understand why I was so upset.

"Thanks, hurry please," and I ran back down to the clinic to help Becky. Kyle and his winning personality joined us shortly after Hal arrived.

"I don't know what the big deal is guys, I think you are overreacting to it," he yawned as he leaned against the wall.

"Over-reacting? Are you fucking kidding me right now Kyle!" I yelled. I was so angry I couldn't hold back my tears; I didn't want to show any weakness, so I walked to the back of the clinic to regain my composure. This was the second time I'd shed tears there. Kyle saw how upset I was and followed me to the back. The last thing I wanted was for *him* to see me crying. I'd already had that big run-in with him, and I was not in the mood for another. I expected he would continue to show disrespect for me and interpret my tears as nothing more than a "typical girl" overcome with emotion and not thinking clearly. In reality, they were tears of utter frustration and anger. I was tired of Becky's and my legitimate concerns being brushed off as an over-reaction. We had faced that response from almost day one of arriving at the camp on Bagram and even more so once we got to the firebase.

Surprisingly, his reaction was quite the opposite. "Hey, listen, I'm really sorry Jenn," he apologized, "I didn't realize how upset this made you guys."

"Listen Kyle, you need to understand something, this stuff is no big deal to you, but we aren't Special Forces; we don't go out and get into firefights with the bad guys. We're two Air Force medics, in a place that we had little training to deal with…and that's ok, we've adapted. But, when I say we saw something concerning, it means I know what we saw and I know how uncomfortable it made us feel. My 'over-reaction' is a reasonable and appropriate way to react to what just happened and I am tired you making me feel like it wasn't."

"Ok, I get it," he tried, but I wasn't done.

"I'm going to tell you again about the situation we're in down here every day when we are seeing these patients. There is almost *no* security being provided. The pep talk you guys gave the guards hasn't done a damn bit of good, and I know each and every patient that walks through that door may very well have a bomb, a knife, or something worse. And no one seems to give a damn! So, Kyle, if I have nothing else to rely on for security other than my intuition, you damn well better believe I am going to listen to it!" I was shaking.

"I understand and I can't blame you for that at all. The good news is, these men didn't have weapons and we have several other guys out searching the area they were in for anything suspicious. I agree they do look different than the typical patients we see. Don't worry we'll handle it," he explained.

"Thank you, I appreciate that," I said and took a deep breath, collected myself and walked back to the men in the treatment bay.

My uneasy feeling never went away. I performed an assessment of the patient, and he was completely normal, with normal vital signs, normal mental status and no injury to explain his symptoms. When I asked the man when he became "unconscious" he could tell me the

CLOSE ENCOUNTERS OF THE TALIBAN KIND

exact time he passed out and for how long he was out. This was interesting because not only do the Afghan people in that area have no real sense of time (most don't even know how old they are), but this was a classic sign of a patient faking a syncopal (fainting) episode.

I decided to start an IV on the man and give him some plain normal saline. "Hanifi, tell him that I'm going to give him some medicine to make him feel better," I instructed, and he did. The man nodded… and *amazingly* after not even 100cc's of salt water his ailment was cured.

While the normal saline was infusing, Curtis came down to assess the situation. "I agree that these men are not from this area. Looking at the way they're dressed I wouldn't be surprised if they're from Pakistan. It's interesting for them to come to us when they would have passed through multiple areas with much larger treatment facilities. Let's get Ivan down here to question them." After several minutes Ivan appeared and questioned the two men that accompanied our "patient" and discovered they lived in a faraway region, under very heavy influence of the Taliban. They maintained they knew nothing. They were questioned for an hour, fingerprinted and released. Our newly "cured" patient walked out of the clinic a "new man." We closed and locked the door after they were gone. Clinic was closed. Becky and I looked at each other in disbelief of what just *could* have happened, hugged, and walked up to our rooms and shut the door.

CHAPTER **26**

Day 93
A Different Kind of Wounded Warrior

31 July 2008

Causalities of war had become our norm; I learned to expect it on a daily basis. A stab wound, a gunshot wound, or perhaps another victim of an RPG. It was just another part of my day in Afghanistan. How funny, considering back in the safety of the United States these types of scenarios were so far from the "norm." My reality had become the opposite of everything I was used to treating on a day-to-day basis. Medical conditions had taken a backseat to traumas.

Today reminded me that illnesses were still a part of the new world I was living in. Ivan had not been feeling well all day. He was complaining of generalized abdominal pain and nausea throughout the day that appeared to intensify as time progressed. I had given him an antiemetic (medicine for nausea) but it didn't seem to touch his symptoms and by the evening, his symptoms became significantly worse. He was out in the common area dry heaving with a slight fever and nothing I was trying was helping. I instructed him to lie on his bed so that I could perform an exam.

I took his vital signs and saw that his fever was continuing to increase and his abdomen was very tender. I pushed on the right lower abdomen and he about came off his bed as he winced in pain.

A DIFFERENT KIND OF WOUNDED WARRIOR

I performed a heel tap, which is an exam that consists of tapping on the heel and seeing if there is a reaction of pain due to the motion that it caused in the abdomen. When patients reacted to such an exam it was a tell-tale sign they had what we in the medical community call an "acute abdomen," meaning he likely had a severe infection or pathology going on.

When I hit Ivan's heel, he complained of excruciating pain, and I felt confident in my diagnosis. My concern was he had developed appendicitis, and he needed surgical attention as soon as possible.

"Hal, I'm very concerned Ivan has appendicitis. We need to call a medevac to get him to TK as soon as possible," I said.

"I'm on it Jenn," he answered and ran to the OpCen while I finished with Ivan. I met up with Hal at the OpCen and we made the call to the FST. I spoke with the surgeon and expressed my concerns. After the arrangements were made, I sat with Hal and explained why I'd come to the conclusion I did and explained to him the importance of a detailed note to send with our patient as he was transferred to the crew on the flight and the surgeons at TK.

Despite poor Ivan and his agonizing pain, it was an opportunity for me to mentor Hal on what to write in a medical note and acute abdominal pain. He was so receptive and appreciative to all that goes in to making a medical decision, such as the one I had just made. That moment with him made me appreciate how our worlds had come together and how we were able to learn from each other. I'd spent so much time and energy in school learning all about medicine, it had become my passion. Hal, on the other hand, had studied so much on how to treat trauma in his training with the team. As we packaged up Ivan, I couldn't help but smile as Hal continued to ask me questions on appendicitis.

Ivan was such a trooper through the whole thing. While he waited for the medevac I could see his pain was worsening by the minute. When I offered him pain medication, he refused, "I want to make sure my symptoms aren't masked by medications. I want the surgeons to have no doubt on what they need to fix…this is miserable."

"I understand, but this wasn't a hard diagnosis to make Ivan, plus I'm sending a detailed account of how everything happened," I asserted.

"No...I'm good, I can take it," he insisted. As we loaded him on to the bird, I folded up the note I had written with Hal, which contained the details of his vital signs, the medications and doses given, his physical exam findings, and my assessment and plan and put it on his chest.

"Good luck, you are in great hands with these surgeons...I know them well," I said as I squeezed his hand knowing he might not return to the firebase before I would be leaving.

Several hours later I called back to the FST to find out what the final diagnosis was. Sure enough, it was an acute appendicitis and Ivan went into surgery shortly after his arrival at TK. He did very well during the procedure and throughout his recovery. He later told me he would never forget the experience and was thankful we were able to get him out of there. He said his fondest memory of the whole ordeal was his recovery. He said the FST loaned him a pair of scrubs, and when he was able to get up and walk around, he made it his mission to go around TK and raid the connexes for fresh fruit and bread to send back to us; knowing our living conditions were subpar compared to where he was.

CHAPTER **27**

Day 98
The Best I Could Do

5 August 2008

With just under two months left on the firebase I found myself extremely homesick and missing Greg more than ever. I knew today he was on a solo bike trip on the Harley to Washington D.C. to visit a friend and see the sights. I longed so much to be with him, seeing such important landmarks in our country's history. I knew I would leave this deployment and this experience with a profound appreciation for what we as Americans have in the United States.

Even the clinic was wearing on my spirits. I wanted so much to reach out to these people, but frequently found myself so frustrated day after day by the limitations I faced in the care I could provide. On an almost daily basis, I would face someone that would absolutely be a hospital admission or a surgical case in the United States. I remember seeing one man who traveled for five days by camel to see me after his arm was blown up in an explosion. He had it wrapped in a dirty cloth and as I took the bandage off I couldn't believe what I saw. The muscle and skin of his entire elbow was destroyed. It appeared to be covered with a yellow salve that had been applied to help keep it clean. I could see the exposed fractured bones and felt such sympathy for this man, knowing he needed attention I could not provide. Hal and I cleaned the infected wound as well as we could, gave him IV and oral antibiotics and pain medication. I called TK and my friend, the orthopedic Surgeon, and told them about the man. They agreed to treat him so I sent him and his camel on their way in hopes he could get the surgery he needed. He was so grateful for what little we were able to do and he promised to take the medications as I had prescribed and would start on his dangerous journey to the surgeon.

Amazingly, the man did arrive to the clinic five days later. My friend informed me he would never regain function of his arm, but at least they were able to save it. I couldn't begin to count how many children I saw with acute asthma exacerbations or pneumonia and severe dehydration that needed hospitalization. The majority of their parents, if I was fortunate enough to see the parents, were so terrified of the Taliban they refused the trek to TK for more definitive care. The sad reality of the people around me often became overwhelming.

I treated a two-year-old girl who had "fallen" three days before, and her father stated she hadn't walked since. "Why didn't you bring her to me as soon as this happened?" I demanded.

"He say he wasn't there when she fell," IG translated. As I looked at the girl, I discovered her leg was swollen, red, and tender to the touch. She screamed in pain with the lightest touch to the area. I sedated her so I could perform an exam and treat her injury.

Based on my initial impression, I was concerned she could have "compartment syndrome," which is a medical emergency where the muscle compartment has too much pressure that causes compression of the nerves and blood vessels and can cause tissue death. I was reassured this was not the case once I got my hands on her. Luckily she was neurovascularly intact, meaning her blood vessels and nerves were functioning as they should.

I tried to get an x-ray of her femur, but of course the portable x-ray machine was not working; yet another setback to face. As I touched her thigh, I felt her femur literally crunch and move under my hand, mid-shaft and down toward her knee. In the United States, this would require an urgent orthopedic consult. She would likely need surgery,

THE BEST I COULD DO

or bed-rest with a special cast as a minimum. I had nothing but fiberglass and an ace wrap.

I tried to tell the father this, and he insisted he could not make the trip to TK for proper treatment. They would have to make do with what I could come up with.

"Sir, I don't have the proper equipment here to treat her appropriately," I tried. "If you don't take her to the surgeon she will likely lose some functioning of her leg."

"He say he understand and is grateful for any help we can give," IG translated. I managed to splint her with a make-shift cast in the form of a stirrup and a posterior long-leg splint.

"It is very important you keep her leg as immobile as possible and in the 'cast' for at least eight weeks," I explained.

"He does not understand what you mean, he does not understand the calendar in the way you say," IG said. I had to find a different way to give him instructions so I found a piece of paper and drew fifty-six hash marks.

"Sir, every day I need you to mark off one of these, and when you get to the last one you need to bring her back to me," I instructed. The man nodded that he understood. I gave him a bag of pain medicine and antibiotics and directed them to the door. As I watched the father walk away, carrying his daughter, my heart ached. I wished so much I could do for them what I would be able to offer in the United States. Thankfully, eight weeks later, the father retuned with his daughter. He informed me he kept his promise and did not remove the splint. As I began to unwrap it, I was overwhelmed with the scent of urine and fecal waste. It was completely covered in filth. Once I got it removed and she relaxed enough for me to touch her, she realized she no longer had pain and was able to move the leg and she was even able to bear weight on it. I tried to explain basic rehab techniques to the father; I am sure he did the best he could.

Dealing with stories such as these on a daily basis was literally draining. I found my sanctuary in running. There was a track the team had made by shoveling rocks out of the way to form a path around the HLZ. It was very close to the size of a 400 meter track back home and I found myself frequenting it on an almost nightly basis. I was running distances I never attempted to run back home, which was certainly something I was proud of. I had to be careful not to roll my ankle on the large rocks, but it was my only escape. Often times my friend "Rod" (his first name was Greg), who was an Army dog handler, would come out to the track as well with his dog Jacko to train. I think it was his escape too. It became almost a routine to run by them and wave with each lap. The day-to-day was taking its toll on all of us, and we were all coping with it in our own ways.

After clinic was over that day, and after my run, I went back to my room and watched a documentary that Greg told me about on YouTube, done by the National Geographic Channel on the Green Berets in Afghanistan. I watched in awe at the accuracy of the documentary's depiction of our conditions. Everything that happened to the team they were filming had happened to me on this deployment, whether directly or indirectly with our team; from traveling in a convoy at night, to the MedCap, to dealing with the radios, IEDs, or the reality of losing a friend to combat. I couldn't believe I was actually in the middle of it all; unbelievable. I had no choice but to push through and do my job.

I looked at the clock and shut off the documentary, realizing it was time to man the radios while the guys left for another mission to find another IED and head into hostile territory in hopes of finding some bad guys. I prayed their night would be unproductive and that they would all come home safe…it was the best I could do.

CHAPTER **28**

Day 104
The Little Big Things

11 August 2008

Without a dining facility our food options were limited. We could eat what the local nationals prepared which most commonly consisted of rice and beans over naan, MREs, or what we stockpiled from care packages sent to us by our loved ones. Due to the inconsistency of ring flights to the firebase, we rationed our food from the care packages to ensure we would have enough to last until the next delivery, but we often ran out. Tuna and peanut butter became staples for me, and I was always thankful to Greg for sending as much as he could.

Becky and I would often trade food with the guys, depending on what they had, and we quickly developed relationships based on our "bartering." Our friend Rod always had the good stuff like candy, chips and crackers, and sometimes some dry roasted almonds. He was always so generous with his treats and we quickly developed a bond over our goodies. He would frequently come to our room with his dog Jacko and hang out with us while we would tell stories of home and savor our snacks. After clinic today Becky and I were sitting in our room talking when we heard a knock on the door. It was Rod with a huge smile on his face.

"Hey guys! Guess what? I just heard we're getting a food drop today!" he said.

"That's awesome!" We were so excited. I hoped we would get some fruit, but that was often wishful thinking; regardless, it was a welcome piece of good news.

"I'm going to help pick it up at the Drop Zone, do you wanna help stock the storage sheds?" he asked.

"Heck yeah! That means we get first dibs on the good stuff!" Becky said. We hurried to the OpCen and waited for the first load to arrive. After about an hour the guys returned and Rod called over the radio for us to meet him and help unload the ATV. We hurried to the shed to start sifting through what we got. We were excited, but when we opened the first box, Becky and I never imagined how happy we would be to see fresh vegetables. There were heads of lettuce, some onions, and green peppers.

"Becks!" I screamed, "We can make a salad!" I couldn't even remember the last time I had eaten a salad; one of my favorite meals back home; a rare treat here.

"Oh wow! Quick Jenn! Grab enough for us to make one and let's stash it in our room before someone else gets it," she said.

"You got it!" I squealed as we scrambled to gather our ingredients.

Rod couldn't help but laugh at the two giddy school girls standing in front of him. "I just so happen to have some dry roasted almonds and ranch dressing in my room if I can get in on that salad," he said.

"You had us at almonds," I laughed. "We can throw in some tuna and…. look! Here's some provolone!"

We hurried through our duties stocking the shed over the next couple of hours. As soon as we could, the three of us broke away. Rod went to his room, grabbed his almonds and dressing and we snuck into our room and had our feast. All three of us giggled and talked as we ate. Poor Rod suffered through hearing about clothes and decorating ideas that Becky and I had for our houses when we returned. He was a great sport and chimed in with his own tips.

"Well ladies, I prefer to shop for all of my décor at Bass Pro Shops, but that's just me!" he joked. We talked about ideas for gifts to give our husbands and what he could buy his wife. A simple, carefree conversation over a salad with friends was such a rare treat. It made me forget the realities of the situation we were in. Sometimes such little things in life make a huge difference.

CHAPTER **29**

Day 106
Out of my Hands

13 August 2008

With every day I spent in Afghanistan, and the more war I saw, the more I longed to be home. Two days before, the team had a mission to go into a very hostile area where the majority of the people were members of the Taliban or their supporters. They were expecting to get into a firefight, which of course was worrisome for me; every time they went out we worried one of them wouldn't come back.

Naturally as the guys left, Becky and I took our second job of manning the radios. Throughout the day we listened in horror as they got ambushed several times by the Taliban. It was the worst feeling, hearing the gunfire in the background as they requested Close Air Support (CAS). Back at the firebase, two of the team guys stayed with us and were hanging [shooting] mortar rounds as requested by the team commander to help with defense of their position. As previously planned, CAS targeted several pre-determined locations in effort to draw the Taliban out. One particular compound, that was said to be a safe zone for some high ranking Taliban, was demolished with a 2,000 lb. bomb. Unfortunately the Taliban had time to flee the compound before the explosion, and before they left, they forced eleven civilians to remain in the targeted compound. Eight innocent lives were lost and three people were wounded. After the blast, the team had the task of digging the bodies out of the rubble. I couldn't imagine how this must have felt. Hal told me later they were buried holding each other; women holding babies, men holding women, it was awful.

The three injured civilians were evacuated and brought back to the clinic where we treated their wounds. While we cared for them, some of the guys questioned them and discovered one of the survivors, a man, was a facilitator for the Taliban. He was paralyzed from the waist down. His wife had minor injuries, and thankfully their baby only suffered minor injuries as well. The rest of their family had perished in the explosion. I couldn't imagine how it must have felt for them to have their lives completely flipped upside down and lose the majority of their family, not to mention being cared for by the people who were responsible. War is a horrible thing.

Along with the surviving family came a little boy with his five-year-old sister, who was not in the same compound but one nearby that was hit by a mortar round. The little girl's nose was cut badly and appeared to be broken. The whole time I was treating her, she kept crying, "I am only hurt a little, I am strong! I am ok!"

"Tell her she is so strong….she is so brave!" I pleaded with the Terp, holding back my own tears. I wanted so badly to take her into my arms and hold her. I wanted to make all of the terrible things that happened there go away, but I couldn't. All I could do was suture up her wounds and treat her pain.

Luckily, our guys fared much better through the whole ordeal. Two of the ANA soldiers were wounded, one was shot in the back, and thankfully the round did not penetrate his body armor. The other soldier was shot in the hand and we later air evacuated him to TK. The incident made national news and I can't describe how it felt reading about myself, and the people I was with, on the internet. The whole thing got to me; it was horrible to see what happened to innocent people who did nothing more than frequent the wrong place at the wrong time.

The next morning I woke up, well-rested and in a somewhat better state of mind. I went to the clinic and saw yet another child on the verge of death due to severe dehydration and malnutrition. At least with this little one her father agreed to take her to a bigger facility to get more definitive treatment; this certainly was not the norm. Death was an everyday circumstance to these people, it was like the majority of them seemed numb to it. Later in the morning I saw a sixteen-year-old boy who had crashed his motorcycle three days before. He was the nephew of an ANP soldier I had treated throughout the month of July for a gunshot wound to the leg. He'd come to see me every day for dressing changes for almost a month after returning from the FST. He thought highly enough of me that he brought his entire family for care several days before he brought in his nephew; I was grateful and happy to help in whatever ways I could.

When I saw the boy I knew the situation was not a good one. He was originally treated by the bazaar doctor nearby. As I lifted the boy's pant leg, I could see what this "treatment" consisted of. He had a "splint" made of four small twigs, about the diameter of pencils and blue cloth. While this was certainly not the standard of care in the US, I had no idea what I was in for just beneath this configuration. As I cut away the cloth, I saw a large glob of hair that was soaked in egg. Apparently it was thought that this combination had some healing benefits. The odor took my breath away and the idea of touching the hair and egg was almost too much. I felt my stomach turn with nausea.

I put on another pair of gloves and took a deep breath and began to cut it away from his skin. After quite an ordeal of cutting, I was finally able to get the hair and egg off and performed an x-ray which unfortunately revealed a serious injury. He had a comminuted (broken in multiple places), displaced tibia fracture with a segment of bone millimeters away from puncturing his skin. His fibula was also fractured. This was, without a question, a case for an orthopedic surgeon. He would need the kind of intervention that I could not provide, and of course his family was unable to take him to TK because his father had no money and feared if he made the journey the Taliban would kill him and his son. I called and spoke with the orthopedic surgeon, who recommended external fixation, which I did not have the equipment for, so he talked me through how to reduce the fracture and we came up with a make-shift treatment plan together. I splinted him in a long-leg cast for four weeks. Then he was to return, and I would place him in a short-leg cast for four more weeks, and there could be absolutely no weight bearing on the leg for the entire eight weeks. I explained to the boy and his father he would likely lose some function of the leg, but he should still be able to walk. I sent them away with my new calendar system of hash marks feeling I did the best thing for him, given the circumstances I had to deal with.

After clinic I went up to my room and shopped online for Griffen, my stepson. He was coming to live with us in Florida and would be there when I got home. This was a huge step for us as a family and I wanted to send him a little "Welcome Home" gift from me since I couldn't be there to greet him in person. After an extensive search I found him a little bouquet made of candy that was placed in a neat little ceramic shoe. Perfect. I couldn't wait to see my little guy…and Greg. It put a smile on my face thinking about my boys and my life away from this place.

And, just when my spirits were up again, there was a knock on the door. "Jenn! Becky! We need you down at the clinic, there's a little girl who got blown up and she lost her thumb and part of her hand!" Hal yelled.

"Oh my God! How awful, we're right behind you," I said and quickly gathered my things. When I got down to the clinic I saw a beautiful little girl who was covered in blood and had shrapnel wounds to her entire abdomen, face and arms. She had nothing but mangled remains of what used to be her right hand.

"What happened to her?" Becky asked the father.

"She was outside playing and the next thing she knew her hand was blown up!" the father explained and IG translated. As we stabilized her, and made her comfortable with pain medication, I noticed how distraught her father was. He appeared genuinely concerned for his daughter; a rare sight in my experience with Afghanistan.

I put my hand on his shoulder and told the interpreter, "Tell this man we will do everything we can to help his daughter."

"Thank you," he said.

"You have a beautiful daughter," I replied.

He looked at me and began to cry as he said, "Yes, but they ruined her! Her hand!" I looked at IG who could tell I didn't fully understand what the father meant.

"In Afghan tradition, a woman with a mangled hand is undesirable and will never marry, except to a man that is much older," he explained. She was fourteen. My heart sank.

We worked to get her air evacuated out, but the weather was far from favorable for the flight. The visibility was significantly decreased and given the hostile area we were in, which prevented any movement until it cleared. We would have to keep her overnight and keep her stable until we could get her out to TK. Hal, Becky, Kyle and I agreed to take shifts throughout the night with her. I wrote out the schedule of times she would need repeat doses of her antibiotics and pain medicine and we started our shifts. The night was long, but thankfully with the hard work of our team, she remained stable and comfortable throughout. My shift was scheduled at 0200 hours and as I sat in silence with the poor little girl and her father I cried for her. She would likely lose her hand and had already lost her potential for love; she was so young and innocent of all that was happening around her. Her father was sitting next to his child rubbing her hair softly with a broken heart and crying sincere tears of sadness for his only daughter.

Days 107-111
A Father's Struggle

14-18 August 2008

The next morning we were able to get the little girl on a helicopter back to TK for further care at the FST. While the night was relatively uneventful, as she remained stable, it was such a relief to get her to the surgeons who would do the best they could for her hand. I called later that night and was informed they were able to salvage part of her thumb and fingers. They had a good prognosis for her and stated they would continue to follow her progress there.

Two days after this news I was in the clinic and I looked outside and saw the girl and her father walking up to the door. "What are you doing here?" I asked the father.

"We have been released and they told me to take her to you to change her bandages," he answered. I found this to be odd, considering I had just spoken with her surgeon who told me a different story. As I took off her dressing, I saw that this was certainly not what was recommended. She still had pins in her fingers and her thumb was turning black; a sign that the tissue was dying.

I called the FST and was told the rest of the story. The orthopedic surgeon didn't want to discharge her yet, but the father insisted on going home to check on his family, but promised to be back in three days for continued treatment. The surgeon was equally concerned about the status of her thumb. I went back to the clinic and spoke with the father, "Sir, you have to go back to TK, her thumb needs immediate treatment."

He saw my concern and agreed to return. "Yes Doctor," he said, "I will get her back tonight." I changed her dressing and sent them on their way.

Two days later the father showed up at the gate. "Please help me! I was given a letter at my shop in the bazaar that said they would kill me if I continue to come to you," he pleaded with the guard. "I'm scared to travel to TK and I need help."

"Go home, get your daughter and the letter and come back and we will help you," Kyle instructed. Luckily there was a flight coming in later that day from TK we could put them on. Several hours later he showed up empty handed and told the guards he couldn't leave that night and requested to speak with me the next morning. He left before I could speak to him. The next morning I was told he showed up several hours before the clinic opened and was told to come back but never did. I never saw him again.

Several days later I called the FST to see if they heard anything about the girl and her father and fortunately they managed to make it back on their own for further treatment of her hand. The surgeon had to go back into surgery and debride (cut away) the dead tissue of what remained of her thumb, but she did well. I prayed they were safe and she recovered well; however, I never found out, because that was the last update I received.

CHAPTER **30**

Day 112
Reality Check

19 August 2008

I woke up to the sound of gunfire and explosions. I had become somewhat used to the sound, as we got attacked more and more frequently due to the time of the year. I thought initially it was the guys doing routine test fires, yet when we got a knock on the door from Kyle, telling us the base was being mortared, the reality of the situation became obvious. We were under fire all morning, receiving a total of fifteen attempted rockets, luckily for us, their aim was way off. Clinic of course was cancelled, so Becky and I spent the day on the radios.

After our daily afternoon meeting, I went to my room and not five minutes later there was a knock on the door. It was one of the guys telling me there was an emergency patient down at the clinic. I grabbed my things and ran down to the clinic to find a twenty-two year old girl with a gunshot wound to the head. I was told that it happened around 0800 hours, during the time our base was being attacked. I looked at my watch and noted it was 1700 hours.

She was covered in a blanket and when I unwrapped her head I couldn't believe what was in front of me. Her wound was mortal; she had extensive amounts of brain matter protruding from her head and her pupils were fixed and dilated. Her condition was imminent and I knew there was nothing I could do to help her. She was already brain dead and basically, her vital functioning was keeping her body alive.

As we worked on her, I watched her father who was sitting at her side. I was taken aback by the coldness and lack of emotion in the behavior he displayed. He didn't even request to be near her. Eventually I became very angry at this display of what was to me a total lack of humanity. After we finished bandaging her wounds I couldn't stand it anymore. "Hanifi, tell him to sit down by her, hold her hand and at *least* console his dying daughter," I said angrily. I explained everything that was happening to him and then asked if he had any questions.

"Yes, I have one. Is she going to be ok? Her husband is upset," he answered coldly. I couldn't believe a father had such disregard for his own child.

"Sir, do you understand the extent and seriousness of her injury? She is dying. Her body will keep her alive for a short time before infection and her organs will start shutting down," I explained.

He shrugged his shoulders and replied, "Ok. If she dies, then she dies."

I was disgusted by him, and the more I sat there, the more upset I became. Hanifi must have sensed my anger. He put his hand on my shoulder and said, "My sister, this is my country."

I looked at him with tears in my eyes and replied, "It's awful."

He nodded and went on, "My two brothers were killed by the Taliban as well."

"Hanifi! Are you serious?" I gasped in disbelief.

"Yes. They were ambushed and both shot in the head. Jennifer, I watched them both die just like this poor girl."

"I'm so sorry Hanifi," I replied. It took everything I had to keep myself together and not break down into tears. I couldn't understand how these people had come to live so complacently with this horrible reality.

The team conducted their standard interviews with the husband and the father. I looked closely at the husband, trying to discern if he expressed any grief, but he appeared to be handling the news just fine. I noticed his right shirt pocket was overflowing with cash. This was customary when there was a loss of a wife or child to give the husband money to help him move on. We eventually released the girl back to them and said there was nothing more we could do. Even if we could medevac her, there wasn't anything further that could be done for her at this point; she had been in her current state for over eight hours. We instructed the men on ways to keep her comfortable in her final hours and sent them home.

As I walked back up to my room I reflected on the innocent young Physician Assistant I was before I came here. I had minimal exposure to anything *significant* as a provider; my biggest struggles were dealing with uncontrolled Diabetes and Hypertension, or perhaps the occasional strange psychological patient. I never thought this type of scenario would be something *I* would encounter. I couldn't help but wonder if I would ever be able to get these countless *significant* medical encounters out of my head when I returned to my world of "normalcy and safety".

CHAPTER **31**

Day 113
A Day in the Life of a Green Beret

20 August 2008

Just when I thought I couldn't feel worse about this war, after dealing with the incident with the girl the day before, this day happened. The team had intelligence about the Taliban and decided to go out on a mission to pursue the information. As they prepared for departure some of the guys laughed as they listened to what they called their "theme songs" for missions. Doug's song was "The Final Countdown". He said he wanted to go out listening to that song "just in case" it truly *was* his final countdown. Another guy made a joke about making sure his boots were clean so they would look nice for his memorial service. Others, like Rod, preferred to listen to songs like "Simple Man" as he left, which helped him find the meaning in why he was doing what he did. Regardless of how they chose to prepare themselves to go, it was something they each had to do over and over again. As I watched them leave the safety of the gates, I couldn't even begin to imagine what they felt time and time again.

Shortly after they left they got into a TIC, which we handled like every other one they had been in. As we listened intently to what was happening, and performed our duties as radio operators, I heard Kyle's voice on the radio, "Requesting medevac for US Special Forces member! 9 line to follow." I felt chills go down my spine as he read off the battle roster number, which was a way of identifying who the individual was by the first two letters in the last name and last four numbers of the social security number; it was Manuel. Becky and I stared in silence at the radio. Kyle went on to describe his injuries, "Be advised patient has GSW to left thigh with noted exit wound through the right lower back. Currently bleeding controlled. Patient stable. How copy?"

"Jenn, oh my God! That sounds really bad," Becky cried.

"I know Becks, I know…" My mind instantly began to run through the anatomy and what could have possibly been damaged based on the path of the bullet. I knew his injury could be significant; the abdomen and lower back house a large number of vital structures and organs. Then I began to think of his horrible jokes, my birthday party he threw with the ponchos and sombrero, and of course the "Danger" cologne he continued to wear every day. He was often the one to find a way to make us smile when no one else could…I was speechless with worry for my friend.

Thankfully, he remained stable in the field and he was evacuated within thirty minutes of the injury. Hal later told me that up until they loaded him onto the helicopter he continued to laugh and joke speaking his characteristic profanities. This was typical Manuel and hearing this offered a sense of comfort. He was flown directly to TK where the FST could get him into surgery to stabilize his injuries. I called later and was informed he was stable but suffered from a perforated bowel and severe bruising of the sacral nerve plexus and therefore was unable to move the left leg. He was sent to Germany for further surgical intervention and eventually flown home to the States to recover. An update I received almost a year later was he was still recovering, relying on a cane to walk but eager to get back out to the field.

After Manuel was safely evacuated, the team continued to take fire for several more hours. We continued to monitor their radio traffic listening and waiting for any update we could receive. Sometimes just hearing the voice on the other end alone was enough reassurance to give us hope they were ok. As they were finally beginning their way back to the base we began to feel a sense of relief, knowing the mission was almost over. Then I heard the words, "ALCON [All Concerned], be advised VICTOR-1 has hit an IED. I say again, VICTOR-1 has hit an IED." VICTOR-1 was Vehicle One; I quickly looked on the Task Org chart to see who was on the vehicle and realized the passengers were: Kyle, Ben, Curtis, Eric (the Air Force Tactical Air Control Party Specialist, also known as the TACP) and IG. Becky and I stared at the list in shocked silence. I felt a sense of panic; all of the feelings I experienced when Travis died began to resurface. I couldn't help it; we lived, played, ate, and even shared toilets with these guys. We had become a family. We had no choice but to do everything together on our tiny firebase in the middle of nowhere. We were all each other had for the time we were there.

We waited in agony for a status update, forced to speculate on the worst possible scenario as we anticipated the injuries. "Do you think they are going to medevac or try to get the guys back to us?" Becky asked.

"It'll depend on the injuries, but let's start thinking through how we'll handle the patients if they come to the clinic. Think about the types of injuries that could happen with this and we can talk about our plan to manage them," I said.

"Ok, I am running through where to stage them and the supplies we may need now," she answered. We had come up with a streamlined system of how we handled traumas over the last couple of months.

"Perfect, I want you to have airway, breathing, circulation on your mind as we see them come through the gate," I instructed. This was a priority list of care we all learned on the very basic level of treating emergent patients. While it had become second nature to us, it is always a good idea to remind ourselves of the basics.

Finally, after what seemed like hours, the medevac request came. Kyle had a possible tibia/fibula injury; Ben (who had been the turret gunner) had a "spinal injury" with complaints of left leg numbness. The tears welled up in my eyes. It seemed as though the guys I had spent the most time with here were the ones getting injured. Kyle and I had our differences, and we battled them out on more times than I would have liked, but he was still part of the family, he was my "bully brother". No news on Eric, the Captain or IG. I again felt an overwhelming sense of helplessness wishing there was something I could do to help, but all I could do was wait.

The medevac came and took both Kyle and Ben out. Due to the possible spinal injury of Ben; they bypassed TK and were sent directly to Kandahar, a bigger facility. We later heard Kyle suffered from a fractured fibula and Ben appeared to have a back spasm and Traumatic Brain Injury (TBI). They would stay for observation for several days to weeks. What could have been going through their heads as they had to leave the rest of the team after already suffering from one loss earlier in the day?

The entire front of VICTOR-1 was gone after hitting the IED; after looking at the pictures, showing the extent of the damage, it was evident how lucky these guys were that nothing more happened. The vehicle was not recoverable; therefore, they had to destroy it in the field which required permission from the Command Post. This request unfortunately was not answered in a timely manner. The rest of the team was forced to secure the remains of the vehicle for several more hours while they waited for authorization for the demolition.

"Are you kidding me? They have to sit there with a big fat target on their backs while they wait for someone all the way back at BAF (Bagram Airfield) to tell them it's ok? That's crazy!" Becky yelled.

"God, I hope they get an answer soon. You know Curtis, Eric, and IG are still out there," I said.

"Jesus," Becky said. After several more hours, the authorization was granted and the rest of the team finally made it back safely to the firebase. I ran up to each and every guy and gave him a hug, as tight as I could. As Doug took off his helmet, he realized he'd been shot in the head with 7.62mm round. It was wedged in the left side of his helmet, the tip of the bullet had just barely pierced the inside lining of the helmet.

He looked at me and laughed saying, "Better not tell the wife about this one."

I couldn't even speak. He then pulled off his vest and showed me where he got shot in the side plate of his armor. I looked at him and gave him another hug. I remembered the advice someone back at BAF gave before we left about not wearing the side plates, saying they were just extra weight...thank God Doug wore his.

"Don't worry Jenn," he said, "We're fine."

My last conversation with Travis resurfaced in my thoughts; he told me the same thing just days before he died. As they offloaded the vehicle I looked for the other guys injured in the explosion. I found Hal and ran over to him to ask what happened.

"What's the status with Eric, IG, and the Captain?" I asked.

"Eric and IG are fine; they were in the back of the truck and suffered minimal injuries. I treated them in the field."

"Thank God," I replied. I saw them shortly after our conversation and did a quick exam and completely agreed with Hal. Shortly after I was done with them Roy came over and asked to speak with me.

"Jenn, I need to talk to you."

"What is it Roy?" I asked.

"The Captain. He needs to be evaluated, but it's going to be difficult to get him to sit still. He's still out there trying to direct the guys."

"Do you know what his injuries are? Where was he sitting in VICTOR-1?"

"He was in the passenger seat. While we were waiting for the medevac I heard him complaining of elbow and knee pain. He told me his head hurt and I saw he had a nosebleed."

"Wow, that's not good. I need to see him ASAP."

"It gets worse Jenn. I talked with some of the guys and they say they saw him walking around and spouting out orders, when they asked him later what he meant, he didn't remember it happened."

"Can you get him to me?" I asked.

"Let me see if I can get him to calm down. I'll be back," he said and walked away.

A DAY IN THE LIFE OF A GREEN BERET

Roy was finally able to convince him to get in to see me, and he was right, I did have a difficult time getting him to sit down and be evaluated, but I finally did. His knee and elbow were minimal soft tissue injuries, no fractures or dislocations. The nosebleed, which was initially quite a concern to me, thankfully turned out to be no more than a bloody lip. I performed a MACE assessment on him, which is a tool we use to determine whether or not the individual suffered from a TBI. Depending on the initial results, it can be performed over several consecutive days which is vital in making the diagnosis; a TBI can initially be masked, but over several days the condition can progress. When I sat down with Curtis that day his score was ok, but over the next several days his symptoms became more apparent. This progression made it very easy to determine in fact did have an injury and needed further evaluation.

"No way, I'm not leaving the team," he insisted, as I informed him I was calling for a medevac to get him to Kandahar for a CAT scan of his head.

"Curtis...seriously? Let's be real here...you're getting worse every day. Your confusion and memory loss are getting worse, look at this," I showed him his score on the MACE assessment that clearly showed change.

"Damnit! Ok. I get it. I'll go," he surrendered. We got him out that same day and thankfully the scan was normal and within a week he was back out at the firebase with instructions on conservative treatment for his TBI.

We continued to offload the vehicles and mend the cuts and bruises the guys endured during the day. As we took the gear off the vehicles the bullet holes and casings were an unavoidable reminder of the events that occurred several hours before. It was continually being demonstrated to me as each day passed that it takes a special breed of person to want to be in Special Forces. I admired their courage, but it served as a source of constant worry for me. I was so thankful that despite the casualties we had, the guys were all still alive and the only death we suffered that day was that of VICTOR-1...may she rest in peace.

CHAPTER 32

Days 116-117
My War Within

23 August 2008

Ramadan starts at the beginning of September and lasts the whole month. This is a very significant time for Muslims, and therefore the Taliban, a radical Muslim group. They begin the month fasting, to show their devotion to Allah, which leads to inner reflection and self-control. This typically means fighting comes to a halt during this devotion. That said, the days prior to the start of Ramadan, and just after it's over, tend to consist of heavy fighting due to the Taliban knowing they are about to enter into a significant cleansing.

Over the past several days, violence had become more prevalent and had hit its highest level of intensity since my arrival at the firebase. Almost nightly we were getting attacked with RPGs, mortars, and small arms fire. It was an indescribable feeling to be going about normal day-to-day business one minute and then in the next to be hearing gunfire, explosions and rockets impacting all around you. Becky and I would habitually retreat to the OpCen to operate the radios and security camera while the guys manned the walls of the firebase and the mortar pit to defend the base.

The first night we were attacked, during this predicted time of increased violence, we were caught relatively off guard; involved in our normal tasks of the evening when the bullets and mortars began. We scrambled to our areas of responsibility; Becky had control of the camera while I rushed to the radio. Over the span of an hour I could hear the bullets hitting the very wall that was separating me from the chaos outside. The guys were able to fend them off and eventually the firing stopped. After the small slip-up that left us vulnerable we made quick adjustments to prevent it from happening again.

The night of the 22nd we were ready. We stood on the roof with the interpreters listening to the Taliban voices on the scanner talking back and forth about their plan of attack. It was an eerie feeling to hear their voices. It made me so angry knowing they were plotting to kill us, but it prepared me for what was about to transpire. As soon as they began firing, I ran inside the OpCen and directed the camera to see if I could spot their location and tell the guys where they were. I scanned the camera over to a common location that I had learned they liked to attack from.

Sure enough, I could see five to six people firing AK-47s at us. I grabbed the radio and yelled, "Mortar pit, be advised! Location of insurgents with effective fire spotted. Standby for the ten digit grid!" I found the coordinates and called them over the next transmission. "I've got the laser on them for a visual, do you copy?" I yelled.

"We copy, hanging the round now," the voice answered. Seconds later I watched the explosion on the camera and, as the dust settled, I could still see movement and I began to feel my blood boil with rage. I wanted every last one of them dead.

"Mortar pit! Be advised I still see movement. I say again, there is still movement!"

"Roger that, hanging another round," they answered, and the second explosion followed. This time, no more movement. The attack continued for another three hours and I stood in the OpCen in absolute disbelief of everything that just happened.

I'd never been a person to *hate* or want anything bad to happen to anyone, but that night, when I saw them firing at us, every negative emotion possible seemed to fester inside of me. All of the hate they'd brought to Afghanistan, the depression, the poverty, the brainwashing, it made me so *angry*. So angry in fact, that at that point if I had been on the wall with the guys I would not have thought twice about firing my weapon, especially after losing three of our brothers due to *them*. I realized in that moment of reflection just what war can do to a person, and it was scary.

I was always telling Greg how I could not understand how people could actually bring themselves to kill another human being. But as I watched one of the Taliban men I located on the camera (who was clearly wounded from the first mortar round) move slowly to grab his rifle, I had no hesitation in telling the guys to hang another round, and I found an unexpected need to watch the man stop moving and it felt good. Who had I become?

The next morning was the first time in three days we had clinic and regretfully it was the saddest day I had dealt with yet. The numbers of patients had dwindled down to almost nothing, due to the locals' fear to be around the base during such a violent time. Our first patient of the day was a little boy about ten years old who came in with a black cloth slung over his shoulder, like he was carrying a sack of potatoes. It clearly had something in it and when he came inside he plopped it down on the gurney and opened it up. I looked inside and saw he was actually carrying a tiny baby. As he pulled out the lifeless child I knew it was a terrible situation. The baby was his six-month-old sister. As he unwrapped her I looked at her tiny body and realized it was too late for me to help; she looked like nothing more than a skeleton with skin. Her pupils were fixed and dilated, she had blood coming out of her rectum and she was agonal breathing (medical term for the type of breathing you see in a patient in the last minutes of life). Hal and I couldn't believe what we were seeing, a tiny innocent body trying to stay alive, but we both knew her little soul was already gone.

I looked at the boy, as tears welled up in my eyes, and asked him how long she had been like this.

"Since she was born," he answered emotionlessly. I looked at him in disbelief.

"Why didn't you bring her to us sooner?" I asked. He simply shrugged his shoulders.

"Well what made you bring her today?" Hal asked.

"My parents told me to, so I did," he replied.

"She's dying....minutes from now she will be gone. It's too late for us to do anything to help her. You need to take your sister to her mother so she can spend her last moments with her," I said. He nodded without any visible sign of emotion. He put her back in his "sack" and without remorse slung her over his shoulder like garbage. He looked at us and gave a slight nod of the head, turned and walked out. Hal and I looked at each other in shock and the tears started to flow from our eyes.

We had just witnessed a scene so devastating it even brought a Green Beret to tears. It was by far the most disturbing thing I'd seen in this country. We hugged and consoled each other through our tears; it took several minutes to pull ourselves together to continue to see the rest of the patients that had come in.

If that wasn't enough, a man brought in his son who had fallen down a hill earlier that day who had been to see the bazaar doctor. His face was still covered in blood and dirt with bandages just placed over the filthy wounds. His eye was almost completely swollen shut. I looked down at his arm and saw another splint with hair and egg to his wrist.

We cleaned the area and confirmed with x-ray he had a distal radius fracture (a wrist fracture). We properly applied a cast to the arm and as I was explaining to the man how to take care of his son's wounds, the gunfire began again. It was once again another day of fighting in this war-stricken country. We closed up clinic, ran up to the OpCen, took our positions, and the process started all over again.

My God I was ready to go home.

CHAPTER **33**

Day 121
Running for my Sanity

28 August 2008

Several days ago, an Australian Special Forces team joined our firebase family. Their purpose in being there was to augment the team with several upcoming missions targeting the Taliban. In the short time they were with us I was impressed by their focus and professionalism. I watched them train constantly with their aggressor canine by having one of their team members dress in Taliban clothing, which had been confiscated from a compound on a previous mission, and letting the dog attack. This was a drill used to get the dog familiar to the scent. They constantly drilled on potential scenarios; it was quite remarkable. They also had a bomb dog of their own; a black Labrador retriever named Sarbi. Her trainer worked with Rod and Jacko several times to familiarize them to the terrain.

The night of the 27th they had a joint night operation that was under the Australian command. We were all called to the gym for a pre-mission briefing and as we sat and listened to their commander brief us on how the operation would take place, I couldn't help but stare at them in awe. They seemed to be so motivated and intense, and for lack of better words…high speed. Each of the team members had their faces painted in camouflage and each man carried himself with a sort of bravado that was impressive. As I looked around the room I sensed I was not alone in feeling this sentiment. They carried out their mission on foot, which was even more remarkable. The unit as a whole was on top of its game and happy to help in any way. I felt a sense of security knowing we had so many extra people to help defend the base. Luckily, the first of several missions were a success and everyone returned without a scratch. This, of course, was a huge relief. I'd already seen far too much of the aftermath of combat and did not care to see anymore.

Clinic had been relatively uneventful, which was always a relief. With the down time several of the Aussies came down and spent time with us. Their medic, named Will, volunteered to see patients with us. It was nice to get to know him and hear him talk of his life in Australia. His mate, Johnny, tagged along when he could. He had an interest in becoming a medic and wanted to learn as much as he could.

As I previously mentioned, running had become my way to vent my frustrations and fears. It was the time of the day I looked forward to the most. I frequented that dirt track at least four-to-five times a week. I would zone out to my music and thoughts of home, letting the day melt away. It was about 1730 hours and I decided it was cool enough to start my run for the day. As I was finishing up the third mile, of my typical five mile run, I saw Hal walking towards the clinic. I could tell something was wrong, so I took my headphones off. "What's wrong?" I asked.

"There's a patient at the clinic, but I think I can handle it. If I need you I'll come get you."

"Ok, you know where I will be," I said and plugged back in to my music. Sure enough, after completing my fourth mile, he came back out from the clinic and got me.

The patient was a young man, no more than twenty years old, who was recently discharged from a hospital in Kabul after having some sort of abdominal surgery. His father brought him to us for help and they were standing just outside of the c-wire surrounding the firebase, next to a van they had driven in. The guards and several of the team guys were already outside talking with the father. The young man was laid out on a bed made of wood and moaning in pain.

As I pulled up his shirt I saw he had a vertical midline incision that extended across his entire abdomen and three small tubes that were covered with dirt coming out of his skin at various points. I assumed the tubes were their version of perhaps a colostomy bag, urinary catheter, and some sort of gastrointestinal tube. The patient looked very ill and his wounds were filthy. He was clearly in no condition to have been discharged from the hospital and I explained this to the father.

"My son was discharged because the hospital did not have any room for him," he said.

"What procedure did he have?" I asked, but couldn't get him to answer. "Sir, your son is very sick. He needs to be admitted back to the hospital for further care by the surgeons who performed this procedure," I explained.

"I cannot go back to Kabul! The Taliban kept stopping me and questioning me the entire journey here," he pleaded.

"Ok then, if you go on to TK, I know the surgeons and I can guarantee your son will receive excellent care," I said, yet he still refused.

"I will still face the same risks along the way, it is impossible."

"There are several other locations relatively close that will be able to provide a higher level of care than our minimal facility. They are not as far and less risk to get to," I tried.

The father continued to decline my offers for help and he began to cry tears of desperation for his son. My heart went out to him as I knew my hands were tied and I couldn't provide the care his son needed. I couldn't call a medevac, I couldn't care for him at the clinic, and I couldn't do anything except offer broad spectrum antibiotics and pain medication. I offered again to call the FST and give them a "heads-up" on the arrival of the man and his son, but the man kept saying the same thing over and over again and I soon realized that I was talking in circles. At one point in the conversation I offered to try to get his son on the next ring flight to TK, but this still was not enough. The father began to raise his voice out of frustration and then made a statement that flipped the switch on my compassion meter.

He said, "Fine! I will leave him here to die then! I can't take him because they will kill me!"

I felt my own frustration levels rising and again I pleaded, "Your son will surely die if he does not get proper care." I tried to convince him that taking the risky trip to prevent this from happening was the best option. "Let's look at the options; you have a chance of death on a trip for care that will prevent a *sure* death if your son does not go. The Taliban *might* attack you...or they *might not*, but your son *will* die if you don't get him help."

He continued to raise his voice in frustration and said, "I will leave my son to die." Every time he said that I found myself getting more upset.

"Your remarks are completely uncalled for and I don't appreciate it. I am trying to offer you everything I can to help him! He needs a surgeon...I am not a surgeon!" My voice was rising as well. We continued to argue for several more minutes and I eventually had to cut him off. "Listen...you can take the medication I am offering you, or you can leave it, but this conversation is not going to change the outcome."

He finally agreed to take the medication and some of the guys that were there gave him some money to assist him on his travels. I knew the things he said were out of pure desperation and frustration and I still felt horribly for him. I wished wholeheartedly I could do more for them and I wished they were not forced to take a dangerous journey, but again, my hands were tied. This was the ultimate frustration for me as a medical provider. I couldn't help him, yet help was what I was trained to do.

As I left the clinic I looked out at my track. I decided to finish my run and ended up running the fastest mile I had run to date; fully completing my five miles for the day. As I went up to my room I couldn't even begin to guess what the next day or week had in store.

CHAPTER **34**

Days 126-127
The Worst Day of My Life

2-3 September 2008

It started like any other day, our boys had continued to go out on missions, with the only exception this time being the team would be going with our friends the Aussies again. The briefing the night before warned everyone they would be going into a very dangerous area and so the extra help was certainly welcomed by all. After the meeting, I went up to the roof of the OpCen and had a conversation with Jay, the engineering sergeant on our team.

"So Jay, this sounds like a pretty big mission, how do you feel?" I asked.

"Are you kidding me? I'm pumped! I think this is going to be the biggest fight of the year!" he exclaimed. I watched him pace around me with determination, anger and excitement in his eyes. "I even have a special shirt for the occasion," he bragged.

"A special shirt? Really Jay?" I joked.

"Yeah, it's my 'Screw the Taliban' shirt," he laughed.

"Well, whatever makes you happy I suppose," I said with a smile on my face as I looked out to the sunset. I wondered what the next day would bring. Little did I know his prediction of the level of violence couldn't have been closer to the truth. That night I had radio

THE WORST DAY OF MY LIFE

watch from 0300-0400 and Rod was my relief. He was going on the mission and when he showed up to pull his shift, I tried to convince him to go back to bed and get some rest.

"I can cover your shift," I said.

"No, I need to do my part, just like everyone else," he insisted, "Go to bed, I got this."

"Whatever! You just want to search Bass Pro Shop sales online!" I joked and chuckled with him for a few minutes. On my way out of the OpCen, I turned around and said, "Hey Rod, if I don't see you before you load up, good luck."

He smiled and nodded his head; I could tell he was already preoccupied with thoughts of the upcoming mission.

The morning started off slowly with little happening as expected, but once they got to their destination an ambush was waiting for them as they had predicted. What they failed to predict was the massive number of the attackers. It easily exceeded the hundreds, completely taking our forces by surprise. The radio transmissions from the team were filled with gunfire in the background, making us all back at the OpCen extremely nervous for the team.

"Oh my God, Becky!" I screamed.

"Listen to them," she replied "This is horrible! What the hell is happening?"

As we listened to them call for CAS I could hear sounds of explosions and gunshots, mixed with the pressured and fearful speech of the man on the other end of the radio.

"I need air support ASAP!" he screamed. "We're in real trouble here!" My stomach turned as we listened helplessly from the firebase. The first call came over.

"We have a friendly USSF WIA," he said. As I listened I felt the all too familiar heartache. He listed the battle roster number and I looked quickly at the list hanging by the radio and realized it was Jay. I couldn't believe the irony of our conversation the night before.

"Injury sustained is a GSW to the left forearm," he explained.

Thank God! I thought, *He was likely stable.*

The firefight continued and the team decided they were going to push through to the firebase for the medevac. A sense of relief came over me knowing he was ok, at least for the moment. Ten minutes later we received another call, "Be advised…two friendly WIAs, Australian SF. Injuries sustained: Patient One, GSW to abdomen. Patient Two, GSW to the leg." The gunshots were louder and more frequent in the background and the radio operator's voice seemed to become more panicked as the time went on. Then I realized the voice I was hearing was Curtis. The voice of the team commander, someone I had grown to know as calm, cool and collected now carried a heavy tone of stress and fear. I felt an eerie realization things were going to get much worse. Several minutes later he was back on the line.

"Requesting emergency resupply of ammunition, we are running critically low. I say again, requesting emergency resupply! Over."

At this point the plan had changed to a medevac in the field; the team could no longer wait to get to the firebase to treat the now three wounded soldiers. The area was still very hostile and they were going to attempt to push forward to an area they could secure for the aircraft coming in.

We waited some more. "Firebase be advised, we've sustained another WIA. Convoy will proceed to firebase; ammo levels are too low and cannot obtain secure airspace for medevac. Over."

"That's one, two, three…now four patients right?" I asked Becky, as I looked at my notes.

"That's my count," she whispered. Her eyes were filled with shock and horror.

"Ok, the medevac is going to be rerouted to us; I need to get down to the clinic to prepare to receive these patients."

"I'll man the radios and meet you down there as soon as I get relief," she said. I nodded and ran down to the clinic. I frantically tried to get as much of the hemorrhage control supplies, pain medications, trauma sheers and other supplies into my pockets as I could. I set up the oxygen, opened the pharmacy, and got IV bags ready, put on my scrub top and gloves and waited by the door with my handheld radio.

THE WORST DAY OF MY LIFE

Five minutes later I began to hear gunshots. I looked up and saw them heading for the gate, heavily engaged in a firefight. The next thing I knew, I saw the first HMMWV round the corner with people yelling at me about the wounded patient they were carrying. It was an Aussie who had been shot in the leg and the buttocks.

"Offload him to the ground in front of the clinic so I can evaluate his wounds!" I instructed. I cut off his clothes, assessed his level of consciousness and pain and noted he had minimal blood loss. I determined he was stable enough to hand over to the Aussie medic, Will, who took control of the patient with the utmost confidence. Will would later prove to be an amazing asset during the whole ordeal.

By the time Will had taken over the patient the rest of the trucks were coming through the gate. They all had patients to unload, and what I thought was going to be four patients soon turned into thirteen! There were nine Australian causalities, two interpreters, Jay and then Eric. Eric had minor wounds and was able to wait until everyone else was addressed, which turned out to be a blessing because as the TACP he was heavily involved in talking to the incoming aircraft on the radio.

The most serious injury in front of me was the Aussie with the gunshot wound to the abdomen. Another soldier had been shot in the thigh and lower leg; another soldier had severe shrapnel wounds to the face, chest, and arms, another with a gunshot wound to the arm and leg. It was complete and utter chaos. As I continued to see the patients and triage the new arrivals, I realized what resources I had. I was, as a Physician Assistant, the most senior provider, Will was the most senior medic, and Hal and Becky were trained and ready to go.

All of the uninjured men offered to help in whatever ways they could. Will thankfully had much experience in this type of combat situation and was able to help me manage the chaos. I knew I would need to delegate a lot of the treatment to the medics and oversee the situation ensuring everyone remained stable and that all of the potential complications with trauma patients were avoided. I had to think about pain management, avoiding narcotic overdose, hypothermia, volume loss, prevention of infection by initiating antibiotics and constant reassessment of stability, just to name a few.

As I worked from patient-to-patient, Curtis came up behind me and placed his hand on my shoulder and whispered in my ear, "Jenn, I need to tell you... we have a friendly KIA."

I felt chills run down my spine, but I couldn't stop working, I couldn't let myself digest the reality that one of our own had been killed. I suppressed everything I was feeling and simply said, "Ok," and continued working on the men in front of me. I finally got to Jay, who thankfully was stable and when I saw him he instantly smiled. "Don't worry, I am fine," he said.

"Jay, are you sure? How's your pain?"

"I'm ok, but please, get this fucking 'Screw the Taliban' shirt off of me!"

I couldn't help but smile at him, remembering how he was bragging about it the night before. I promptly cut the shirt off.

"Do you want me to get rid of it?" I asked.

"No!" he insisted, "Just leave it with me here." He pointed to his side.

"Ok Jay," I agreed and left it by his side as he requested. I needed to see that he was ok; it gave me the strength to press through. Once all of the patients I was seeing outside the clinic were stable I found Curtis and mustered up the courage to ask him who the KIA was.

"Who was it Curtis?"

He looked at me with sadness in his eyes and said, "Jenn...it's Rod."

I felt a lump forming in my throat and my eyes tearing up. *Not Rod! My friend! He sits outside with Jacko every night I run the track cheering me on! He laughs and jokes with me and Becky when we get homesick. I just talked to him that morning at shift change. Now he's dead? NO! Not him...not my friend.*

I stared off blankly in a state of shock, my thoughts saturated with the voices of the men I had revered as the most impressive fighters I'd ever seen now screaming helplessly in pain and agony in the background. I felt myself losing it, and immediately turned my focus to the situation at hand. I still had patients inside I hadn't seen yet. I had to keep it together. I walked into the clinic and saw Johnny, the Aussie that had been so eager to learn the medical world was now lying on the stretcher in the first treatment bay. Just two days earlier he was standing in that same room learning some basic medical techniques from me and the other medics, now he was a patient with two gunshot wounds to the leg. He was screaming and breathing rapidly and heavily due to his pain.

"Hang on Johnny! You're going to be ok," I tried.

"It hurts so fucking bad!" he cried.

"Here's some morphine, it should help. I need you to calm your breathing ok?"

"I'm trying, I'm trying."

The medication started to take effect in a few short minutes and he was stabilized. "You guys watch him and keep a close eye on his vital signs," I instructed to the men standing next to him. I walked to the back to evaluate the rest of the patients Becky and Hal were working on. I saw someone lying on the next stretcher that looked like Sola, an interpreter, but I barely recognized him. His face was covered in blood and bandages. He had been shot in the face and also suffered from shrapnel wounds. As I was treating him, I dropped a bandage on the floor. As I looked down to see where it landed, I noticed both of my shoes were soaked in the blood of these men. I thought to myself, *Keep working, Jenn*. I was about to go to the next bay once Sola was attended to, but as I was walking out I looked on the other side of him and saw a stretcher on the ground with a body on it covered by a blanket. I knew it was Rod. I felt I had to pull the blanket back, perhaps for some sort of confirmation he was really gone. Once I lifted the blanket, I couldn't help but notice how peaceful he looked. His feet were crossed and his eyes were closed and he appeared as if he were taking a nap. I could have pretended that was what he was doing if it wasn't for the pool of blood behind his head. He was killed by a shot to the back of the head. I was consumed with a deep sadness for my friend.

I heard voices coming out of the next bay and snapped out of it and hurried into the next room. The patient was Hanifi, my friend and interpreter, who just days before told me the horrible story about his brothers being shot in the head by the Taliban. Now here he was, lying on a stretcher with a gunshot wound to the face. "Hanifi!! Are you ok?" I yelled. Becky had been in the room with him and was tending to his wounds.

"Yes, my sister! I just have a headache," he replied. He was so sweet and I couldn't stop telling him how proud of him I was. Thankfully, his wound was a through-and-through shot to the cheeks and he was stable.

"Becky, keep a close watch on his mouth and the bleeding, he could choke on the blood." She had already thought of that and was standing next to him with suction ready should she need it.

"I got it," she said, and she did.

We had to keep the entire group of patients stable until they could all be evacuated out, unfortunately only three-to-four patients could fit on the helicopters at one time, which meant we would be spending hours with these soldiers until they were safely on their way. I continued to bounce from patient to patient, which forced me to keep walking past Rod, and at times I had to actually step over him. Each time I saw him I had to pull myself together. I had to witness the process of getting him into a body bag; from stripping his clothes off, collecting his personal effects he had with him, to getting the actual bag in the room and finally placing him in it. I saw it all.

It took an hour before the first helicopter arrived. Sola was slotted to be on the first bird out, but at the last minute he was bumped from the flight. As time continued to pass, I grew deeply concerned for him. I figured he had maxillofacial fractures (fractures to the facial bones) and his airway could be compromised at any moment. I put him on oxygen and insisted his vital signs be monitored every five minutes, hoping to avoid intubation if possible. My concern and hopes to avoid intubation were due to the unknown timeframe of the next bird to get him out of there, not to mention the limited supply of Rapid Sequence Intubation (RSI) medications we had and his overall well-being. I had no idea what the extent of his injuries were, but if I had to stick a tube down his throat I was risking pushing a piece of fractured bone that could have broken loose down his airway in the process. Several of the workers on the firebase, who were local nationals and his friends, were standing by him, desperately wanting to help in whatever way they could, constantly changing out his bandages and cleaning the blood from the area around him.

Thankfully, he remained stable and breathing on his own and after an hour of monitoring him, he was evacuated on the next flight out along with my friend, Hanifi. After another hour, the final bird came and the remaining, most stable patients were loaded... along with Rod. I watched as they carried Rod's body out of the clinic and onto the helicopter. It was the last time I would ever see him. As they were securing him on the gurney, Becky and I were standing in the clinic pharmacy. We looked at each other and closed the door. We instantly grabbed each other and shed our first tears of the night. Our friend was dead. Our boys were wounded, some of them critically. I began questioning everything. *Did I do enough? What could I have done differently? Why did this happen? Why are we even here in this country? Why did I have to witness something so horrible?* As we held each other I remembered Eric. Initially, when all of the vehicles were coming in the gate under fire Roy yelled to me, "Don't forget about Eric!" but he had been on the roof for the past four hours on the radio calling CAS and directing the medevac birds. I gathered supplies and went up to the OpCen to treat him.

As I opened the door to the OpCen I saw Ben and Kyle standing there. They both were facing the door with an indescribable look in their eyes. They had made it back on one of the medevac flights. It was so good to see them, yet it was the worst way I could have imagined to be reunited. I gave them both a hug and no words were spoken; there was no need. I quickly headed up to the roof to see Eric.

"Eric, you ready for me to take a look at your wounds?"

"Yeah, I just need to finish this up," he said as he finished writing in his log what had transpired with the flights. After four hours he was still in his full gear; flak vest, weapon, ammo, and radios. All of which easily weighed 50-60 pounds; he did his job so selflessly. I was in absolute awe of the character he displayed that night. I ended up getting an x-ray of his leg because I was concerned he might have a large piece of shrapnel stuck in it, but thankfully he didn't. I did pull out several large pieces from his shoulder. I cleaned up the rest of his wounds and I stapled a laceration on another guy's head together and I was finally done treating patients.

I went to my room, collapsed in my chair and began to sob. This was the worst day of my life. Becky and I sat in silence and soon there was a knock on the door.

"Hey guys, are you ok? I just wanted to check on you," Roy said.

"Thanks," we said.

"Do you want to talk?" he asked.

"No," I said. There was nothing to say. We just sat and cried together. Eventually Becky and I decided to take showers. I looked at my legs and realized that not only my shoes were covered in blood, but I had blood all over my clothes and legs. I knew I could wash it off, but nothing could wash away the images in my mind.

After I showered, Roy offered to let me use his satellite phone to call Greg. As much as I didn't want to tell my husband about what happened, to prevent him from worrying, I knew I had to. He was the only thing that could make me feel better. I took Roy up on his offer and went up to the roof to be alone with my husband. As soon as I heard his voice I lost it. I cried and cried. He was so good and just let me cry. "Nej, sweetie, I don't know what happened, but I love you so much."

"Rod's....dead....he's dead..." I managed between my sobs. I couldn't even imagine what must have been going through his head during the conversation. I couldn't tell him very much detail at all, and what I could tell him probably scared the shit out of him, but he

THE WORST DAY OF MY LIFE

never let it show. He was my rock, which was what I needed at that moment.

After about thirty minutes we hung up. I went to my room and tried to sleep, but couldn't. I looked at the clock and it was 0130. For the first time in my life I took a Valium to knock myself out. At 0300 there was another knock on the door. It was Kyle.

"So, I need you guys to give me the details of all of the patients and their injuries," he said.

"What? Why?" I asked in my foggy haze of Valium and sadness.

"I need to log everything," he lied. It was so draining to have to go through the details again and likely very unnecessary. It was just Kyle being Kyle…just plain shitty. I was too tired to fight him, so I gave him what he wanted. As I recounted the day's events I truly felt numb. I had no more emotion to spare after the day was over, and after reliving the entire event again and he had all of the information he "needed," I fell asleep, and slept until 1100.

3 September 2008

I woke up very somber. As I got dressed, the previous day's events played over and over in my head. When I walked out to brush my teeth, I saw Rod's blood soaked helmet and M4 rifle lying on a table just outside my room. I suddenly felt nauseous and got away from the reminder of his death as quickly as possible. On my way back up to my room I saw his dog Jacko and my tears returned; he looked so lost, pacing back and forth looking for his master. I felt as lost as he did, unsure of how to proceed through the remainder of the day. I soon realized no one had planned a memorial, so I took it upon myself to make it happen. As I was making my list of the things I needed to accomplish, in order to have the memorial, Roy came by, "Hey guys, how're you feeling?" he asked.

"Numb," I answered and Becky agreed.

"Listen, I didn't want to tell you this, but Kyle tasked you guys to inventory Rod's things. They need to go out on the next ring flight," Becky and I instantly started to cry.

"Are you freaking serious Roy?" Becky asked, "Don't you think that is a little out of line considering how good of friends we were?"

"I'm not surprised honestly," I added, "Anything Kyle can do to make things harder on us, he'll do."

"Listen, don't worry. I know how close you guys were so I already handled it. I just wanted you to be aware," Roy assured.

"Thank you, that really means a lot. I don't think we could handle it today," I said. Just the thought of that task took away any emotional strength I had recovered from the limited amount of sleep from the night before.

"No problem at all, I'm here for you guys," he said.

"We're here for you too Roy, we all need each other as we deal with this," Becky said. We gave him a hug and he went on his way. I found it difficult to concentrate. I wanted to honor him properly at the memorial. I had to find his boots, dog tags, rifle, helmet.... *did someone clean it?* Thankfully, after realizing no one had, and seeing how upset I was, Roy took care of it. I had to find a picture, his family's names, Jacko's leash....*would anyone speak? Would I have to?* As the day went on I asked numerous people for assistance in putting it together and became incredibly angry because no one would help, not even Becky. I knew she didn't because she couldn't handle it, but I wasn't so sure I could either. I managed to get it all together and at the last minute Curtis took the reins and spoke. We all dressed in our full uniforms and at 1530 hours we said goodbye to Greg Rodriguez. At the memorial Jacko paced the room constantly until he stopped at Rod's shoes and helmet, smelling them. He continued to search for Rod and smell his boots throughout the remainder of the ceremony. At the end I took a knee in front of his things, said a prayer for him, kissed my hand and touched his helmet saying my last goodbye.

I did feel a sense of closure in having paid him the tribute; I knew he was in a better place and God would watch over his wife and children. I later learned the details of his death. After Jay was shot, the team began taking heavy fire. Rod took it upon himself to protect his comrade by shielding him from the gunfire. While he was protecting him he was shot in the back of the head and died instantly; a hero.

After the memorial service I went down and cleaned and restocked the clinic in preparation for the next day. As I cleaned the rest of the blood off of the beds and the equipment my heart broke all over again for all of the guys. I found myself trying not to dwell on the horrific reality of what happened; instead, I tried to focus on the beauty of the night that had been overlooked. It was truly moving how everyone came together as one to help deal with the horror we all faced. Even the local nationals working on the firebase as cooks and laborers were there helping clean that night, without anyone asking them to. Every soldier who was able to help was down at the clinic lending a hand. Ordinary people had done extraordinary things. It was truly amazing.

I learned from that night that life is precious. We all say that, but I understood the depth of it after that experience. I was thankful for every moment I had and the love I had been blessed with in my life. I knew I was there seeing and experiencing all of this for a reason, I trusted that. I prayed for the strength to get through the rest of the deployment and to get home safely. I knew I'd changed through this experience; I prayed the change was all for the better and my experiences would give me the strength to endure the life ahead of me.

The men involved in the mass casualty all made it. Hanifi and Sola later returned to the firebase after Becky and I left. The Aussies all recovered, the soldier shot in the abdomen sustained the most critical wounds but survived. Jay suffered from a broken ulna (arm bone) and underwent surgery and they were able to recover the bullet in his shoulder. Rod was buried at Arlington National Cemetery and his final wishes were granted; Jacko was flown out on the next ring flight and was retired to the Rodriquez family.

I have included an article that was printed in the Washington Post after Rod's burial, in honor of his memory:

166 DAYS

By Mark Berman
Courtesy of The Washington Post
Tuesday, September 16, 2008

When early reports suggested that Gregory A. Rodriguez was a hero who took a bullet that would have struck another soldier, those who knew him probably weren't surprised. He was committed and loyal, someone who could be counted on whenever he was needed, those who knew him said.

Yesterday, Sergeant First Class Rodriguez was honored for his sacrifice in services at Arlington National Cemetery. Rodriguez, 35, of Weidman, Michigan, died September 2, 2008, of wounds suffered in Ana Kalay, Afghanistan, when his mounted patrol came under small arms fire.

His wife, Laura M. Rodriguez, told the Morning Sun of Mount Pleasant, Michigan, that he wanted his final resting place to be Arlington.

"I asked Greg if anything ever happened to him where he'd prefer to be buried, and he told me Arlington, as he wanted to be among the best and the brave," she said.

Rodriguez was the 501st member of the military killed in Iraq or Afghanistan to be buried at Arlington. He was assigned to the K-9 unit of the 527th Military Police Company, 709th Military Police Battalion, 18th MP Brigade, based at Ansbach, Germany.

More than 100 mourners stood before a backdrop of floral arrangements and wreaths to pay tribute to Rodriguez. They joined members of the 3rd U.S. Infantry Regiment from Fort Myer who waited at the gravesite along with four dogs from the same regiment.

A chaplain, Major David Baum, welcomed mourners and talked about the white tombstones around them and the sacrifice they represented, weaving Rodriguez into that tapestry. Rodriguez was buried in Section 60 of the cemetery, along with many other casualties of Iraq and Afghanistan.

Rodriguez's wife and his mother, Virginia Richardson, received flags from Brig. General Jeffrey Phillips.

Rodriguez graduated from Mount Pleasant High School in 1991 and joined the Army Reserve three years later, his wife told the paper. He went on full-time active duty in December 1996, and she said they were stationed in places as far-flung as Hawaii, Missouri, Alaska, Texas and Germany.

Rodriguez, a military police dog handler, was part of a special search team with his dog, Jacko. The dog survived the attack in Ana Kalay, and Laura Rodriguez said she hopes Jacko will be released to the family.

"He was Greg's best companion for the past couple of years," she said. "He'd been sleeping with Greg every night since they landed in Afghanistan."

Greg and Laura Rodriguez were married in Honolulu in 1999 and have three young children. "Greg is the best dad, a loving husband and an awesome soldier who loved being able to train and handle his K9 companions," she said.

Rodriguez was a Detroit Red Wings fan who enjoyed hassling other hockey fans, she said. He was "a very committed, loyal individual," but he also had a special sense of humor.

"Greg loved to push everyone's buttons and get people going with his rare, unique sense of sarcasm," Laura Rodriguez said.

Rodriguez's sister told the Detroit News that her brother was committed to keeping order. "My brother liked to be the law," Lisa Dombrowski said. "He liked justice. If it wasn't right, he made it right."

She said her brother was so skilled at training military dogs that he was given the most difficult ones, and that when other trainers couldn't get a dog in shape, it would be sent to Rodriguez. And she said he usually got the job done.

CHAPTER **35**

Day 129
My Grieving

5 September 2008

The days after the mass casualty were slow. Everyone seemed to need the time to recoup, including me. I did see patients the day after, but after clinic was over I kept to myself for my own grieving process. A flight came in and we all said our goodbyes to the remainder of our Aussie friends and Jacko. I was sad to see the Aussies go, they were a great group of guys and I would never forget working with Will. He was an absolute stellar medic and an outstanding soldier. It was also hard saying goodbye to the dog. We had all grown to love him as part of the family. He loved working with Rod, and it showed. I will never forget how he would carry his harness in his mouth before a mission because he was so excited. It was interesting to see the notable change in his behavior after Rod's death. He seemed lost; desperately searching for his master.

Thankfully, when the Chinook came in it was carrying six new team guys to help augment the firebase. They had been in place at a different firebase, as part of a different ODA team, but were able to come and lend a hand. We had lost so many people to injuries; the team was down to five Special Forces members from the original ten. The new guys seemed nice and I was sure they would fit in well, but

I didn't have much interest in getting to know them. I found I was slowly distancing myself from the team and the other people on the firebase as a defensive mechanism. I felt homesick and completely worn down emotionally.

The Chinook also brought back one of the Aussies from the team that had been medevac'd with minor injuries. He was Sarbi's (the Australian bomb dog) handler; during the ambush Sarbi went missing and they were unable to find her before they left. Because she was a bomb dog a lot of money had been invested in her training, but she was also a part of their team and they wanted to do everything in their power to bring her home. Of course they feared the worst; that she too was killed in action like Rod.

After clinic I was searching the internet and saw the story of what happened on September 2nd had made international news in both America and Australia. Seeing this reminder of the severity of what happened, I sunk even lower into my grief. But in my moments of solitude after that horrible day, I began to realize how important it was for me to tell the story of these men and their sacrifices. It saddened me to know that we, the citizens of the United States, had little to no idea what actually goes on in war and we should. The things that used to stress me out seemed so petty now. I remembered the "girly girl" I was; someone who was so scared to get off the plane at Bagram Airfield in April, a place that now seemed like a sanctuary compared to the firebase. I realized over the course of my deployment I'd grown leaps and bounds as a person.

CHAPTER **36**

Day 132
New Hope

8 September 2008

    This was a much needed good day for me. Clinic was actually a positive experience; far from the norm I had grown to expect. For the first time I saw a husband who appeared to genuinely care for and love his wife. She was seven months pregnant and complaining of low back pain. After ensuring she was not in labor I talked with them about the low back pain that can come with pregnancy. As I gave them educational information on how to relieve her pain, I realized they probably had never seen anyone before for prenatal care. "Would you like to listen to the baby's heartbeat?" I asked. I watched their eyes light up with excitement as they heard the interpreter translate my question. They both nodded enthusiastically. They held hands as I put the gel on her belly and put the Doppler on her skin. At that moment the baby kicked and I watched the man squeeze his wife's hand. When I located the baby's heartbeat I watched them both smile from ear to ear. What a huge moment it must have been for them both, especially considering the region we were in and its lack of medical care. They both thanked me profusely for the rare opportunity.

    As I walked the couple out of the clinic, I saw an old man with two walking canes, his ankles splinted in permanent braces suggestive of a neurological disease such as cerebral palsy or a similar condition. As I walked up to him I said "Shalom (Hello in Dari)," as I did with every patient.

And much to my surprise he replied back in English, "Good morning, how are you doctor?"

"Well! Good morning to you sir!" I said, pleasantly surprised to hear him speak English, as I always was with any patient there I could speak directly to. We talked about his medical complaint, which was an infection in his prostate and when I finished discussing the treatment plan with him, I asked, "Is there anything else I can do for you today?"

He looked at me and said, "Yes doctor. Now I will ask you a favor."

"Ok," I said, skeptical of what he would request.

"I am on a quest," he explained. "You see, once I learned to speak English it became my mission to teach it to as many children as I can."

"Wow, that's incredible. Are you teaching students now sir?"

"Yes doctor, I have fifteen pupils now. My problem is that I don't have any supplies to teach with, and that is my request of you."

"What do you need?" I asked eagerly.

"If you can spare some pencils, paper, and any other school supplies I would be so grateful," he said as he put his hand over his heart. As I listened to his request, my heart filled with respect for this man. It was so rare to see anyone in that area with much education and even more unusual to meet someone who wanted to have a positive impact on the youth.

"Wait here, let me see what I can do," I replied. I hurried up to the OpCen and asked for help from the guys who were ultimately responsible for that sort of thing. I walked with them over to the connex, where they kept their humanitarian aid, and made sure the man got as much as we could spare. When we gave him the supplies, I could see the gratitude in his face.

"My heart is filled by your kindness," he said as he started his

NEW HOPE

journey home with his two canes and bags full of school supplies on his back.

"Tashikor," I replied and bowed my head.

I also got to see a little boy for the very last time that I'd been treating for several weeks for a partial finger amputation. He was about five years old and was working at home and got his little hand caught in a grinder, resulting in his almost losing several of his fingers. I had to actually remove the end of one digit because it was so mangled. I instructed him come in every day for dressing changes saying, "Now listen sweet boy, I need you to come back every day and let me change your bandages. But, you have to keep this clean ok?"

"Yes doctor," he would say. Like clockwork he returned every day, covered in dirt. He did what he could to follow my directions, but he couldn't avoid his living circumstances. Thankfully, with the daily dressing changes and antibiotics we were able to keep the wound clean. He was very sweet and seeing him became one of my only things to look forward to in clinic. I would watch him march up to the clinic in his bare feet holding his hand up as if he was trying to prevent it from getting any dirtier than it already was. He would see me and wave with his good hand and smile. As we changed the dressing each day, I could see it was painful, but he did everything he could not show that it hurt.

"Do you need me to stop for a minute?" I would ask, as he winced in pain.

"No doctor. I can do it. I'm strong man," he answered. He was indeed a strong little man and I would miss him. As I said goodbye to him the final time I gave him as many things as I could to help him; toothbrushes, toothpaste, soap, a winter hat and coat, etc. I would never forget his courage; he never once complained, so very brave.

Lastly, I saw a very interesting Dermatology case that was worthy of writing a case study about when I got home. After I got as much information as I could from the patient, I researched my differentials of diagnosis as much as possible and sent an email with pictures to my friend Chad, a dermatologist I met in my training. I truly found the case fascinating and was excited to proceed with my plan of care for the patient. I hoped I would see him throughout the course of treatment before I had to say goodbye to the clinic and firebase for good. It felt so good to be excited about medicine again. For the first time in several weeks I felt a piece of *me* was still there, and that was a great feeling.

Unfortunately, after several days of searching, the Aussie who returned to retrieve their missing bomb dog, Sarbi, had no luck in finding her and sadly he had to leave without their teammate. I prayed that night for the dog, that if she was alive, she was not in harm's way.

CHAPTER **37**

Day 134
Shut Down

10 September 2008

It had become significantly obvious that Becky and I were no longer the scared, naïve, and sheltered women we were when we first came to the firebase. We'd become something I never thought possible; numb. We were sitting down in the clinic after we had finished seeing our patients talking.

"I feel like we're so removed from everything and everyone," Becky said.

"We are. I really don't care anymore Becky."

"I don't either, what's the point?" Before Rod's death we couldn't wait to get back up to the OpCen with the team and be a part of the group, but now we didn't want to be involved with anything. By sitting in the clinic we were trying to get away from it all by talking, laughing and sharing stories of home. As we sat, we heard the all too familiar "boom" of an attack. The Becky and Jenn we used to know would've jumped in shock and fear as we heard the sound, scurried up to our positions, and waited for further instruction; the two hardened ladies we'd become sat in the clinic and barely flinched. *Who cared? What can they possibly take from me that they haven't already?* We knew our place during any attack was to be in the OpCen, while the team took the wall and defended the firebase…but we sat.

"You think we should check and see what's going on up there?" I asked.

"I guess so," she answered. We eventually opened the clinic door and looked up toward the OpCen and saw the majority of the team standing on the roof looking off into the distance. The attack was occurring at a checkpoint just outside our firebase.

We both sat and watched in our detachment; neither one of us cared. At one point as the booms continued, I opened the front door to the clinic that the patients normally enter through, and stood outside with my arms in the air with clenched fists. "Come on God! What's next? Bring it!" I shouted. I was daring Him to take me. I didn't care what happened at that point. I'd officially shut down.

When the attack was over, and it was deemed safe to exit the clinic, we went back up to our rooms and Hal told us that one of our ANA soldiers at the checkpoint had been killed. The Jenn I used to know would've been upset, shaken, and saddened by the loss. I didn't know who that person was anymore; she was gone. I listened to him tell me the news. When he was done I nodded, gathered my things, went to my room, closed the door and went to bed. Sleep would make it all go away. It was the only thing that could.

CHAPTER **38**

Day 135
9/11

11 September 2008

On September 11, 2001 the most horrible terrorist attack on American soil occurred, and we were all never the same. I, like every American citizen who was old enough to remember, will never forget where I was that day. I was a young Airman working on the Medical/Surgery (Med/Surg) floor at the Nellis AFB hospital, having served just over one year of active duty time. For some reason around 6am PST (9am EST) I couldn't sleep so I called my friend Ron to talk. Ironically he was up as well. We made small talk and then I turned on my television; we both fell silent as we watched the second plane hit the World Trade Center. I couldn't believe what had just happened. I hung up the phone, put on my uniform and rushed into work. We all gathered in our break room and watched the rest of the horror unfold on television. After several hours those of us who were not scheduled to be on shift, were released to go back to our dorm rooms if we lived on base. We agreed to get ready in case we were needed to help in whatever ways we could in New York. There were specific disaster teams that were in place in the event something like this were ever occur; the members trained frequently on scenarios that would require an immediate response for assistance, but there was no way to prepare for this type of tragedy. Being as young as I was in my military career, I had not been assigned to such a team, but the majority of my colleagues were.

I remembered the drive back to my dorm as if it happened yesterday. Lines upon lines of vehicles were stopped at the gate to the base due to the lockdown. As I sat in traffic I stared out the window at the other drivers and watched their faces. They were all the same; wide-eyed and distant gazes of shock, horror, and disbelief. None of these people were speaking; everyone was looking straight ahead in silence. That night I tossed and turned in bed. I'd laid out my uniforms and my go-bag was ready. I wanted....*needed* to go with the disaster team to help, so I stayed up that night writing a letter pleading to my flight chief to let me be a part of the disaster team. The next day I reported directly to his office, letter in hand, and tears in my eyes begging to go. I felt that I *had* to help.

"Sir! I know I'm too new to be on a team, but please consider me as a volunteer willing to step in if I'm able. I will take anyone else's spot who doesn't want to go. Please…I am begging you."

"I appreciate your heart, Airman" he replied, "I will keep you in mind if any opportunities open up on the team."

"Thank you, sir" I said and walked away. It was in that moment I felt for the first time that my purpose in the military was bigger than me and my selfish reasons for joining. Despite being ready and able to help, the disaster teams Nellis AFB staged to depart at a moment's notice were not needed.

I sat on the roof of the OpCen and reminisced about the eager and motivated Airman I was on this day seven years ago. Now here I was in Afghanistan feeling completely defeated and numb to the violent world around me. That fire, that heart, that motivation to make a difference, was all in my far distant past. I wished I could meet that young naïve person and spare her heart from the harsh and brutal realities of war, but I couldn't. Instead I knew I would live those realities for the rest of my life.

September 11, 2008….so what? Just another day in this hell.

CHAPTER **39**

Day 142
Falling Apart

15-18 September 2008

As the days passed, it became clear the firebase family had fallen apart. It was very tense and everyone seemed to be on edge. I found myself withdrawing more and more and spending every day preparing myself to leave. No one wanted to talk about feelings and seemed to avoid addressing the issues at all cost. Many attempted to go on as if nothing happened; pretending not to have suffered from the loss that we all shared. Becky and I got word we were on the next ring flight out of the firebase which couldn't have come at a better time, I was emotionally exhausted and felt all the joy of my job was now gone. It was time for me to get the hell out of there.

The six members that recently joined us from the other Green Beret team were very helpful; one of them, named Chase, was a medic. He was a nice guy; someone I wished I could've worked with the majority of the time of my deployment, instead of Kyle. He had a good head on his shoulders and not overly cocky like Kyle. All the same, I was ready to leave. I was realizing every day that passed I was shutting down. The night before I was so tired I lay down early but I could hardly sleep at all because I couldn't stop thinking about all of the bad things that had happened. It actually scared me; I'd become so *consumed* with these horrible thoughts that I couldn't sleep. I wondered; *Am I going to be ok after this?* I knew how fortunate I was to have such a strong support system at home, but still I wondered. I knew I'd changed and realized now it was up to me on how I *dealt* with the change.

Ben's condition continued to deteriorate. Apparently there was much more to the injuries he suffered when VICTOR-1 hit the IED that threw him from the vehicle. While he was at KAF he didn't tell the whole truth about his symptoms. He wanted to get back with his team, so he managed to get on one of the medevac flights the night of the mass casualty. He was the weapons sergeant for the team, which was a job that required lifting and maintaining heavy weapons throughout the day. He began to notice he couldn't perform his duties and went to Hal for help. Hal then came to me.

"Hey Jenn, you got a sec?" Hal asked.

"Yeah, what's up?" I replied.

"Listen, I need your help. I just talked to Ben and I'm real worried about him."

"What is it? What's wrong with him?"

"Well, he told me that since he got back he's had weakness and numbness in his left hand. He said he's having trouble lifting things."

"Are you serious? How long?" Ben was the typical SF guy; nothing but muscle, spending the majority of his time in the gym. Weakness was never a word any of us would have used to describe him.

"Since he got back a couple of weeks ago Jenn. What do you think it is?" he asked, genuinely concerned.

"It could be serious Hal; he could have a severe neck injury. I need to evaluate him right now," I got up and started to the door.

"Jenn! No! Wait! He told me that in confidence. He'd be so pissed at me if he knew I came to you," he pleaded.

Normally that wouldn't have fazed me in the least, but this was a different situation. I thought about the determination Ben had to get back to his team despite his injuries. They were family to him. I had to respect that bond; but at the same time he needed attention. I wrestled back and forth with what to do for several minutes.

"Ok, I get it Hal. I do. I will teach you how to do a neurological exam on him, but you have to *promise* me if there is anything at all that you see, that looks abnormal, you have to come and tell me immediately. Do you understand?"

"Absolutely....Jenn, thanks. I promise. I'll take good care of him," he said as he walked out of my room. *Ugh! I hope I made the right call with this,* I thought. I would give them the space they needed, but I had to stay on top of it. It took a couple of days of Hal treating his symptoms before Ben would actually let him do the exam, but he finally did. When Hal came back to me and reported the results they were not good.

"He gets medevac'd now Hal," I insisted.

"Yes ma'am, I'll make the call," Hal said, "I think he's expecting it." He left on the next flight out and returned to KAF for further evaluation. As he was loaded onto the Chinook it dawned on me how much certain individuals can influence a group. He was a great guy and an amazing and dedicated soldier. I thought about the rest of the people who were no longer with us. It seemed the people who'd impacted us in the most positive way, with the exception of Hal, were the ones that were now gone, leaving remaining skeleton of a team in a word - "broken".

When he arrived to the treatment facility, more tests were run and it was discovered he had both a skull fracture and - what I was concerned about - a fracture to his cervical spine. He'd been walking around with a broken neck for almost a month! He wanted so much to be with his team that he put himself at great risk to do so. Luckily, he suffered no permanent damage.

September 18th was my last day of clinic. As I stood in the place that had been my life for three months, I felt sadness. Despite all of the tragic things that occurred right where I stood, I still had some fond memories of the place. I would miss our interpreters and Hal dearly. Hal had come in to his own as a medic in the short amount of time that we'd shared. After everything we'd faced together, he'd become a good friend, one I would never forget. Becky and I shared this sentiment and tried to make the most of our last day. We drank chai one last morning with our friends and tried to have some laughs about some of the memories we shared in the clinic. The interpreters had gotten into the habit of bringing us chai every morning and they knew that this would be our last so they also brought us some cake. They'd given us each an Afghan name; mine was "Nazanin," which meant darling. I thought it was such a nice name to give me so I began writing "Nazanin" on my cup every day instead of "Jenn". On that day, as one of the interpreters poured my chai, the other handed me a marker and nodded to my cup and said, "You will write Nazanin Yes?" I looked at him and smiled nodding my head as I took my cup and wrote my given name one last time.

As we stood together for the last time in our clinic, I looked around at the walls of the building that had become one of the most significant places I had ever been. The few short months we spent there would be in our hearts forever. We found a marker and we each signed the wall with our names and the dates we were there, along with the slogan we'd picked up from the t-shirts they made for us back at BAF, *Good Medicine in Bad Places*. The clinic had left a permanent mark on who I was, I hoped I'd done the same - beyond what I wrote on the wall that day.

Several weeks ago Becky received some pictures that some children from back home had drawn and sent to her. One was of two girls in a field with flowers and trees on a sunny day with two airplanes flying over. We'd hung it, and the rest of the drawings all around the clinic, but that one was our favorite. As soon as we hung it we wrote our names above the little girls and it made us smile every time we looked at it. We decided to take a picture by it, and hoped it would continue to make many more people smile as much as us.

As we closed the clinic door one final time, I thought of all the people I treated successfully and all the people I had to turn away because I didn't have the capability to help them at that facility. I'd learned more in that place than every book I'd read in school and every patient I'd seen back home; both about medicine and myself. I was thankful for the lessons and the people I met, but as I walked away and back up to the OpCen I didn't even think about looking back.

The interpreters and the local labors had worked with us every day and when they heard we were leaving they decided to throw us a party. It was such a thoughtful gesture and they spared no expense. They purchased fresh grapes, watermelon, vegetables, and soda. The cook prepared a delicious chicken curry and rice; a luxury for the region we were in. When we arrived at their hut, I was amazed at the trouble they'd gone to; all of the food was displayed so nicely. I was truly touched by the gesture.

They even went as far as to hire a local musician to play music while we ate. As we listened to him play his instrument some of the ANA soldiers got up and left the room. They returned shortly with their own "instrument"; an old wound irrigation bowl and a lid to the sterilization kit that we'd thrown away in the clinic. They had taken those pieces of our "trash" poked some holes in the lid, tied a piece of wood and string to it and made a guitar.

They sat and played the homemade instrument with the hired musician, while one of the interpreters, Anwari, turned over a water cooler and made it into a make-shift drum. They laughed and played the music while others got up and danced. It was nice to sit and laugh with them as they sang and danced. I would never forget them and how they touched my life.

The next day was to be our last day on the firebase. I was looking forward to a month back at Bagram to unwind prior to going home. I was excited, yet found myself having trouble believing it was truly over. Surely something would happen to ruin it, right? As I lay down to sleep that night tears of mixed emotions streamed down my face. I prayed to God for our flight to go as planned, and to actually leave the scariest place I'd ever been within the next forty-eight hours.

CHAPTER **40**

Day 144
Leaving Hell

20 September 2008

I thought the last day at Firebase Anaconda would never come, but it finally had. Hal was a sweetheart and told us that even though our flight was not scheduled until midnight, he refused to let us go back down to the clinic to work; we'd been through enough and paid our dues. Instead, we stayed in our rooms and packed and talked. As we reminisced on our time there, I wished so many things. I wished we would've had an After Action briefing to help everyone deal with the failed mission. I wished we would've had the support of a chaplain. I wished we had all been more open about how the incident impacted each of us, but unfortunately the reality of the situation was different.

In the early afternoon one of the Afghan soldiers spotted a local Taliban leader in the bazaar right outside of the firebase. After forming a plan of attack at a moment's notice, they successfully apprehended him and brought him back to the firebase. It was a huge catch, which certainly helped boost the spirits of everyone. Once the prisoner was secured and the interrogation began, several of us decided to take a hike up the mountain behind the firebase as a symbol of my last "hurrah" before leaving. I'd been hesitant to do so in the past, but on this last day at the firebase I felt it was almost a *necessary* task to accomplish before I left. We jumped on the ATVs with our M4s and headed up the path to a point and then hiked up the rest of the way to the top.

It was a nice hike and when we got to the top, and looked out over the terrain, I realized what a sight it was; a view of the firebase I hadn't seen before. I appreciated the size of my home for the past three months. It was actually quite small, especially when I saw how vast the area surrounding was. I was amazed so many *big* things could happen in such a small area of land mass.

"Jenn, look off to your left by that ridge line," Hal pointed, "That's the area of the TIC Rod was killed in." Surprisingly I found I was actually comforted by knowing where it happened and seeing the area in a new perspective; I felt a certain sense of closure. As I stood there, with the sun setting over the mountains, I looked down at the firebase, the buildings, the clinic, and the track I ran on every day.

"Hal, can you take a picture of me with the firebase behind me?" I asked and I handed him my camera. I thought someday that picture would mean something significant to me. I had no idea at the time how true that was.

We had our final moments on the top and headed back to the ATVs. As I got on, Hal must have seen the thoughts and reflection in my face; he looked and me and gave me a hug saying, "Congratulations Jenn, you just spent the majority of your deployment in one of the most dangerous places in Afghanistan. How does it feel?"

The only words that I could find were, "It feels like it's time to go home." He agreed and we headed back to the firebase.

After we got back we had one last meeting in the dayroom where the guys presented us with Certificates of Appreciation and a team patch to thank us for everything we did, which was mainly due to Hal insisting we get recognized. It was a nice gesture. They asked us to say a few words and for the first time I was at a loss; the only thing I could manage was, "Thank you....I was honored to have been here with you." I wanted to say so much more, but the words weren't there.

The rest of the evening was spent with last minute packing and goodbyes. I tried to sleep before we left, but I couldn't for so many obvious reasons. I couldn't stop thinking about *everything*. I thought about the first day I arrived, the clinic, the people, the tragedy, the bullets flying over our heads almost nightly, the mortar attacks, the feelings I never thought I could feel, the sadness....the loss. As I lay there, restless in my reflections, someone knocked on our door. "Hey guys! Your flight's delayed one hour!" the voice shouted. I felt my heart pounding....*what if it didn't come? What if we are stuck here another week?* I managed to doze off for about thirty minutes, but was awakened by a loud banging on the door.

"Jenn! Becky! The bird is three minutes out! Get out to the HLZ now!" I looked at my clock; it was right on time....so much for the delay! This was typical of that place; we could never count on something happening as planned or predicted. Becky and I both jumped out of bed and had to scurry to collect our things, get our body armor and weapons on and get out to the HLZ.

As we gathered our things Kyle came in and yelled, "Later Bitches!" which was most likely his way of being "funny," but I looked at him and felt so much anger, disappointment, and relief all at once. I was glad to be finally leaving him in my past, knowing he was someone I was grateful I would never have to talk to again.

Everything happened so fast; we barely had time to get outside, let alone say goodbye. I didn't even get a chance to say goodbye to Hal, the one person I knew I would miss. There were two birds, one for the passengers leaving and one for our luggage. As we finally got situated on the correct Chinook, Becky and I looked at each other in the darkness, knowing we were feeling the exact same things. As the wheels lifted up, and we began to hover over the firebase, I looked down on my home of three months that had filled my heart with some of the most wonderful and most horrific moments of my life and I felt such a plethora of emotions. The most profound was relief, I literally felt like I could *breathe* again. My eyes filled with tears, I knew I would miss the guys; my brothers, dearly. I would never forget my experience there with them, but I was ready to rise above it and move on. I knew it was time to go home.

CHAPTER **41**

Day 145
Back to Reality

21 September 2008

Our travel back to KAF was relatively uneventful, but lasted the whole night. We stopped at Tarin Kowt, and I was able to say goodbye to my friends on the surgical team and a few of the Special Forces guys we'd met along the way. When we finally arrived at KAF it was 0630 hours. We discovered, as we stood on the tarmac at KAF, that the luggage didn't make it with us and was somewhere between the firebase and another firebase along the ring flight. Eventually, after several hours, we ended up locating all of our missing items, except for my hard case. All of my belongings that were important to me from this deployment were in that hard case, if it didn't turn up I would be devastated. I realized all I could do was hope it would eventually show up. I was so tired that my fatigue took over my concern for my belongings; I had to get some sleep.

It was a hard adjustment to be back on a big base, with the big military again. All of a sudden we were wearing uniforms, saluting and following rules and regulations. Even our first meal at a real table, with real food, was an adjustment considering we had lived on MREs and the food our loved ones sent us for the past three months. It felt so strange looking at the HMMWVs and regular vehicles driving on paved roads. As I watched them drive by I remembered my last images of the vehicles on the firebase after the mass casualty; covered in bullet holes, shattered glass and blood. I felt I was in a completely different world.

We were given a key to stay at a B-Hut on the Special Forces camp at KAF, which was assigned to transient medical personnel. We crashed for a couple of hours, showered, and then went to the Med Shed, expecting we would be welcomed back. However, we both felt our reception to be quite the contrary; we were hardly even acknowledged at all. We were not part of *their* group after all, just Air Force augmentees whose services were no longer required. Not to mention the fact that we were *females* on top of it. While the reaction to our return was certainly disheartening, we were still comforted in knowing we were on our way home. During the last months on the firebase, it was so violent that multiple ring flights had been cancelled, which prevented us from receiving mail for almost two months. We decided to ask at the Med Shed to see if any of our mail was there. "Do you guys know if any of our mail is here? We didn't get any for quite some time," I asked.

"Oh yeah? Huh...let me think....there might be some in here," the Doc said and pointed to a closet. As he opened it I couldn't believe what we saw; packages upon packages of our mail from our loved ones. As I looked at all of mine, I recalled the countless days of disappointment we'd shared when our mail didn't come. It was something we looked forward to with all of our hearts; a small piece of home arriving with the sole purpose of reminding us there was a much bigger world out there, beyond the hell we were stuck in. It hurt badly they wouldn't have even told us about them had we not asked, but once we saw all of the packages and envelopes it honestly felt like Christmas.

Throughout the day I ran into several people I'd met along my journey and it was neat to see them again. I even met a nurse practitioner who was likely going to be my replacement at the firebase. As I talked with her I wondered what she would face. *Would she have to deal with horrific situations? Would more of the team become casualties? Will she be ok?* As we parted ways I wished her luck, truly praying she didn't need it.

At dinner Becky and I ran into the chaplain who'd spent a couple of weeks with us at the firebase. "It's so great to see you guys," he said.

"We wish we could have seen you a couple of weeks ago," Becky said as we both remembered the loss of our friend.

"I know. I tried to get back out to you guys after the mass casualty. I know you all needed the support terribly," he said.

"What happened?" I asked.

"Well, 'the powers that be' didn't want to risk me getting *stuck* out there since the ring flights were cancelled so often." I felt my jaw clench as the anger welled in my gut.

"God forbid someone who was so desperately needed after a horrible traumatic event like that gets *stuck* in a place where he could be of the most use!" I snapped.

"I agree completely," he said. "I tried everything I could to get to you guys, but I couldn't make it happen." Everyone on that firebase needed enlightenment and support after that day and I honestly couldn't believe it was not more obvious to those making these *command* decisions. The more I thought about how I couldn't believe that, I began to realize I *could* believe it. It illustrated to me just how far removed and detached from what was really happening on the ground out there these people making decisions were.

As we talked with the chaplain, he began to relate to us, and what we'd been through on a very real level, speaking from his own experience in the past, which helped comfort us. "You should expect it to be hard going home and re-entering into your old lives. No one back home will have a clue about what you've been through and what you've seen and therefore will likely not be of much help," he warned us.

"I know," I said in agreement. "Thankfully I have a phenomenal marriage and an extremely understanding husband who's ready to listen."

"Becky, what about you?" he asked.

"I'm in the same boat. Mike is my best friend and is ready to do whatever he can to help."

"That's good to hear. I imagine where you will have the most challenge coping will be as you transition back in to your work life." I thought of mine and could see why he had the concern. No one I worked with had any idea what I went through and when I returned they would be expecting the same Lt. Clark that left six months ago.

"Here's my phone number and email. I'm always available to talk if you need me," he said as he handed both of us his information. As we talked I could feel myself becoming emotional and ready to cry. I could tell by my reaction, to my first day out of the chaos of the firebase, it would be a slow process to get over everything and get re-integrated into my normal life, but I hoped I would continue to go about it in a healthy way and would lean on my support system. I knew that as time passed the hurt would continue to surface as things became more and more "normal". I prayed for the strength to get through it all.

CHAPTER **42**

Days 148-161
Back to Bagram

24 September-7 October 2008

After being treated the way we were at KAF, we were more than ready to move on and get out of there. My hard case eventually showed up, so we decided to pursue an earlier flight back to BAF and, as luck would have it, we got on one leaving on the 24th. When we landed, it was nice to see friendly and familiar faces from the people we knew before. The journey had come full circle. It was, however, so strange to be back there; it was the same place, yet *we* were so different.

All of the rules that were at one time second nature now seemed ridiculous. We each responded to this change in our own way. I found that Becky and I drifted apart to a degree, not because we didn't love each other and rely on each other anymore, but because we were both *lost* in our own interpretation of how to deal with everything that happened.

Being back at the Med Shed was certainly a new experience. Seeing how the medevacs were being handled had a completely different meaning to us, now having been on the other end of it. Listening to the radio traffic was a whole new ball game. In fact, at times it was eerie listening to the voices on the radio which were once just a voice in the air and now were the voices of our comrades. Every time I heard our team's call sign come across stating they were in a TIC, my heart stopped. I prayed desperately I wouldn't hear a 9-line come across with another familiar battle roster number.

Three days after returning to Bagram we walked into the radio room of the Med Shed and heard a TIC going on with another team. Unfortunately the worst of the worst happened…an IED. The 9-line was called stating there were five casualties, three of which were US Special Forces. My heart sank. As we stood by waiting for the description of the situation the medic came back on stating the 9-line had now changed from five wounded patients to two, and was now requesting three body bags. He called the battle roster numbers and we discovered the fallen soldiers were the engineer sergeant, the weapons sergeant, and the team commander. We later found out the commander just got to the team and it was his first mission. He'd come to the team late because his wife had just given birth to their baby three weeks before. Even though I was out of the "Hot Zone" I was still exposed to the awful realities of war on a daily basis. I now had a clear understanding of what really happens and found myself wishing for the naivety that I had before this trip. I needed to get out of Afghanistan and get home.

Luckily, Tony was still there and was in direct contact with the flights in and out of Bagram. He found out we could leave about ten days earlier than we had originally expected. This was the best news I could have gotten. Sadly, Becky couldn't leave on the earlier flight because she needed to stay in country exactly one-hundred-eighty days to avoid orders to Korea when she returned home. We knew we would have to say goodbye eventually, however, we weren't expecting to have to do it so soon; we planned on parting ways in Baltimore, not Afghanistan. It was sure to be a painful experience for us both.

On 1 October there was a celebration at the clamshell tent for EID, which is the end of Ramadan. I decided to go with the Army Dietician I met at the camp. As I was sitting at the table eating I saw Suraya again. It was so nice to reunite with her one more time before

I left. She felt like a mother figure to me when I'd met her at TK during my time with the FST. I found it so easy to talk to her; we caught each other up on how we'd been, sharing our war stories....literally. She had been out to a firebase with a team for a MedCap. While they were traveling to the set-up location a tractor in their convoy rolled over and caused all of the vehicles to stop. They were stuck in that location for twelve hours waiting for authorization to demolish the vehicle in place due to its being unrecoverable. Because they sat there for such a long period of time, the Taliban was afforded ample opportunity to set up an ambush. The first night the convoy received intermittent small arms fire, but with no damage. They fought through it and got to a more secure location to rest overnight. Because of the firefight, naturally Suraya was scared. The Chief Warrant Officer (CWO) on the team noticed her unease and insisted she sit in his place inside the HMMWV, in the passenger seat, instead of her seat in the open bed of the back of the vehicle, which was ironically the same seat assignment I was assigned on our convoy. She argued with him prior to departure the next day stating she didn't want to take his seat, but he was insistent and she finally agreed.

As they set out on their trip, they once again came under fire. The CWO quickly stood up in the back of the HMMWV to man the machine gun. As he stood ready to return fire he was shot in the back of the neck. The injury completely paralyzed him instantly. The medics had to perform an emergency cricoidotomy (making an incision on the throat, to access the trachea to provide an airway) to allow him to breath. He was eventually medevac'd out. The whole time this was happening, Suraya was locked in the front of the vehicle unable to get out and help. This weighed heavily on her heart. He was in *her* seat; that should have been *her*.

The last update on his condition she heard was that the paralysis was likely induced by swelling around the spinal cord and the doctors were optimistic that he might regain some sensation. She went on to say the last time she asked they told her he'd regained some sensation in his hand. My heart ached for her, but listening to her tell her story was therapeutic. It was calming to speak to someone who had shared in similar horrors. Before we said goodbye that night we exchanged addresses and promised to keep in touch. I hoped we would.

The night of the 7th of October I said goodbye to Becky. Words cannot describe how difficult it was for us both. We'd shared the most traumatic experiences of our lives with each other. We saw beauty and we saw horror. We were alone in a man's world together, sharing everything with them, from their stinky toilets and showers to their triumphs and failures, and their victories and defeats. We touched the lives of the women and children we cared for in ways we both may never realize. We laughed together until we cried and at times we held each other with a raw fear that only the two of us would ever understand. We shared overwhelming sorrow that could pierce the soul. But most importantly, we *survived*....together. Now, we had to part ways and return to the lives that we had before Afghanistan.

"So...this is it huh?" she said as the tears streamed down her face.

"No...Becks, we'll see each other again. I know it."

"Me too. I can't wait to meet Gerg. Give him a big hug for me; tell him thanks for sharing you with me."

"Oh Becky!" I cried. "I love you so much. Thank you for being strong. I can't imagine how this would have turned out without you by my side." We grabbed each other and hugged tightly.

"Back at cha."

"Be safe my friend."

"Yeah...what else can happen, right?" she joked.

"Right." I smiled. "So...see you real soon ok?"

"Can't wait."

We shed many tears that night. As we both turned away to begin our journeys alone. My heart ached for my friend, my sister.

When the overhead announcement finally called for us to load the C-17, I found myself overwhelmed with emotion. It didn't seem possible I was actually putting Afghanistan behind me. As the plane lifted off of the tarmac I felt relief similar to what I felt leaving the firebase, but with a finality that was indescribable. Throughout the

BACK TO BAGRAM

whole flight to Manas I was in utter disbelief that it was truly *over*. No more gunshots, no more mortars, no more missions, no more fear, no more sadness, no more death, and…no more war. For the first time in six months I felt I could actually relax and just breathe; one of the best feelings of my life.

As I dozed off to sleep I smiled; just a few more days in Manas, and then home.

CHAPTER 43

Days 162-166
The Journey Home

8 October 2008-12 October 2008

I traveled out of theatre much the same as I traveled into it. I was accompanied by Tony and Tim again, except we didn't have the same connections in Manas as we did when we first arrived six months ago. Tim's girlfriend already redeployed so we were forced to live in the clamshells like every other transient party. As I stepped off the C-17 onto the airstrip I found myself thinking of the person I was when I first set foot on the same concrete six months ago. I'd been through so much more than I ever could have imagined. I remembered how frustrated I had been with having to wait to use the morale phones, to call home to the family I'd just left. Now, having been through what I had, I found myself in a completely different state of mind. All of the fears in my head when I arrived the first time were now an afterthought. All of my energy was focused on one thing….home.

We stayed in Manas for a total of three days, waiting for our names to show up on the manifest home. While there, I occupied my time with the gym. I decided to put myself on a night schedule to help re-acclimate to the States, since we were about ten hours ahead. I happily turned in all of the gear I was issued there back in April. The days went by relatively quickly; I slept the majority of the days and filled my nights with the gym, email, movies, and time with my own thoughts. Eventually our names were on the manifest out, leaving in the middle of the night on the 11th. As we got on the plane I couldn't wait to leave, hoping I would never return.

We stopped in Incirlek, Turkey to refuel. We were instructed to de-board the plane during the process. We waited and waited to re-board for what felt like hours when finally an announcement came overhead at the airport terminal stating that there was a mechanical problem with the plane and we would be there for at least a night while it was being repaired. There was a unison sigh of frustration from all two hundred plus passengers. We all desperately wanted to get home and twenty-four more hours away was an eternity to us all. Because we were staying overnight we all had to get our orders stamped, allowing us to leave the terminal. After standing in a never-ending line we were all loaded up on buses and were taken to several transient billeting rooms. Once we were all settled, a group of us decided to make the most of our mini-vacation to Turkey and walked over to the BX and purchased a few "adult" beverages to partake in. We did have a good time and some laughs as we all exchanged stories of our time in the desert. I found myself refraining from saying much. As I listened to the stories of the mundane life at BAF and KAF and how people creatively passed the time, I missed Becky, wishing she was there for me to exchange that knowing look with, but I was alone. I found myself in an uncomfortable silence amongst the laughter and jokes. I wanted to be in Greg's arms and put it all completely behind me. I managed to shrug off the looming emotion, put my smiley face on and told some jokes of my own. We stayed up the majority of the night and luckily had a very early call to get back to the terminal; the plane was fixed and ready to go, and so were we.

From Incirlek we traveled to Ramstein, Germany where we switched planes to a more commercial type aircraft, similar to the one we flew in on from Virginia. I'd never been to Germany before; the airport was huge. It was almost like a civilian counterpart. There were Subways, Starbucks, and Duty Frees. People in civilian attire were traveling with their luggage and children just as they did back in the States. As we waited at our gate I saw more and more of these people lining up in the same line I was in. They were flying back to America on standby. As I sat down in my assigned seat, an elderly couple sat down in the row behind me. As they struggled to get into their seat, they bumped mine repeatedly. I heard the woman's voice, "Can you believe this Frank? How on Earth are we going to sit here for this trip? I'm so uncomfortable! I've never been on a plane where the seats were this uncomfortable. Frank? *Frank!* Are you listening to me? I don't have enough space!" She went on and on, all the while bumping my seat as she tried to adjust to her substandard flying conditions. Listening to her complaints appalled me. It was no secret who their co-passengers were; we were all in uniform and it was announced that we were coming back from a deployment. They were still oblivious to this and continued to complain about their *free* uncomfortable seats. I couldn't take it and moved to the back of the plane, put my earplugs in, my eye mask on and slept all the way to Baltimore.

As the flight attendant announced our final descent into Baltimore my eyes welled up with tears. I couldn't control the emotion as the wheels screeched as they touched ground. I was finally back. I couldn't believe it. As I stepped out of the walkway into the airport I felt my knees go weak and I had to sit down. I looked around as the people around us busily walked by trying to get to their gates or to baggage claim and I'd never felt happier about being in an airport. We walked to baggage claim to pick up our belongings and the people surrounding us smiled and nodded in thanks. I'd been in situations before when I was uniform and had a similar reception; however, this time I felt it in my core. The gratitude meant more to me than I ever could've imagined. We stayed the night at the Sheridan where Tony, Tim and I had our final dinner together before we parted ways.

The morning of the 14th of October I couldn't wait to get to the airport. I was going to see Greg again….after *everything*! Griffen was going to be there too, as he had moved to Panama City while I was gone. I was so excited that I was beside myself; I had to go back to my room several times because I forgot things, but eventually made it to the airport. I was in my civilian clothes and blended in with the people around me. No one knew who I was or what had happened to me. I was just another face in the crowd, which was exactly how I wanted it. I didn't want any big reception or attention. All I wanted was my family. I connected flights in Atlanta and realized that in one and a half hours I would be *home*.

I sat in a window seat and as we started our decent into Panama City. I went back to the day I left home, looking out the window with tears running down my cheeks wondering what was ahead. Now, the tears of joy and relief were pouring. The person sitting next to me must have been so puzzled by my emotion, but was kind enough to just let me be alone in my thoughts. As we pulled up to the terminal I couldn't stand it! My heart was beating out of my chest. I wanted to run down the aisle and out of the plane. We de-boarded in what felt like hours and *finally* I was inside. I ran from the gate to the reception area….and there he was.

The love of my life was standing there with a bouquet of roses with tears streaming down his cheeks as he saw me running toward him. We hugged the tightest embrace we've ever had. People around us smiled and could see the love and excitement, imagining how special the moment was for us…..if they only knew! My little Griff was eagerly waiting next to him for a hug and kiss from his stepmom. Words couldn't describe how good it was to see him; I hadn't seen him for over a year. I'd missed him so much and was so happy he was there to greet me. I couldn't take my hands off of Greg. I couldn't believe I was touching him, holding him. I was really *with* him. I wasn't dreaming…this was it. I was finally home.

PART TWO

CHAPTER **44**

The Aftermath

6 December 2009 was the night I realized I was in serious trouble. I looked down at my crying newborn with concern….but I didn't see Ayla. I was holding *that* baby. The dying baby in Afghanistan, whose brother had carried her into my clinic in what looked like a potato sack and plopped her down on my gurney.

As I looked down at my daughter I was right back there, in that horrible place. I could smell the filth in the air, and I could hear the breaths slowly leaving the baby girl's tiny dying body. It was the night of my first flashback….but certainly not my first sign of my Post Traumatic Stress Disorder (PTSD).

Being back was overwhelmingly wonderful and when I first returned home, I found myself thankful for each and every moment I had with my family and in the United States. I had a whole new appreciation for the freedoms and niceties I once took for granted. I remember thinking as soon as I saw Greg I couldn't wait to tell him all the details that I hadn't been able to elaborate on over the phone and through email, but the reality of the situation was I couldn't. I tried several times to tell him, but I found I couldn't put it into words, so I didn't; I still felt an urge to "protect" him from knowing all of the horrible things I went through.

He didn't know how to ask me what I was feeling, so it eventually became a wedge of silence between us. I answered his questions and elaborated on various facts, but avoided discussing my emotions. It made me feel weak. I didn't want him to know I was hurting, mainly because I didn't want my pain to impact him.

I reported to the base to in-process upon my return so I naturally stopped by the clinic. I will never forget walking into my office and seeing everyone. They were so welcoming and eager to hear how I was doing; they wanted all the details they could get. Several new people had joined the clinic since I left and it felt like I was walking into a new place all together.

As I was getting ready to leave, after going through the formalities and hugs, I ran into one of the nurses in the hallway. She was a civilian contractor who'd worked there for years, and was somewhat disgruntled. She gave me a big hug and said, "Oh Jenn! Thank you so much for your service over there! I'm so grateful you made it home safely."

"Thanks, I appreciate that," I replied.

"Believe me; you are so glad you weren't here. It has just been awful since you left," she complained. *Is this conversation really happening?* I thought. "Oh and the referral process! Well, that is just a mess. I just can't believe how broken our system is," she continued. "You are so lucky you were out of here for six months."

As I stood and listened to her rant, I found myself in utter disbelief. Just days before I was getting shot at, my friends were killed and wounded, and she was telling me that I was "lucky" to have not had to deal with the circumstances back home?

"Alright, I'll see you later," I cut the conversation short. I felt rage, but managed to suppress it. I went home and focused on something else to keep my mind from "going there".

Several months after returning to work I was presented with numerous medals and awards, which was typical after a deployment. I remembered how big of a deal that would have been to me prior to the deployment, but now it felt undeserved. I felt I did so little compared to the sacrifice of my comrades. I was carrying tremendous guilt, feeling I should have done more than what I did while I was there. Maybe I could have found a way to better treat all of the unfortunate people I had to turn away. Why wasn't I out there with the team on those missions? It would have made a difference, wouldn't it? I often found myself withdrawing more and more from the things I normally loved; I became significantly more irritable and would often cry for no reason. I would sit in church, listen to the music and just weep. I felt so much hurt, and so alone.

Greg was wonderful, but didn't quite know how to handle my reactions, nor did I know what to tell him. I think we were both in a state of denial of what was happening. I kept feeling if he knew how much I was struggling, he would think I was not strong enough. I felt overwhelmed at times; often feeling lost in a world that was happening around me. Many days I would come home from work, sit at the foot of my bed and just stare off into space with tears streaming down my face. My mind would drift to the memories of who I was before I left; someone with so much passion and drive, filled with a fire for life and optimistic that any and everything was possible. I was so "innocent" to the terrors of war, looking at the world through such a naïve perspective insisting everyone was innately good.

Who was that woman? She felt dead to me. That fire was gone. I was just going through the motions, I felt numb. I left that person and her "innocence" at that firebase, and I missed her terribly. I thought back to who I was before I joined the military, that young twenty year-old, who thought she had it all figured out, but had so many life lessons to learn. So many of the people I met over there were no more than twenty themselves, just starting their lives, and look at what they were going through. Did others leave from deployment in the same condition I had - broken?

Greg told me often that maybe I should get help, but I insisted I could handle it on my own. I told the facts of my story to those who would listen and over time I felt that I had a good handle on my emotions because I learned to avoid them. I learned my triggers and subsequently learned to evade them. I felt so alone; no one could understand where I was coming from or what I'd been through, not even Greg.

Becky and I talked often initially, sometimes needing to talk in the middle of the night when one of us started "thinking too much". Eventually some unfortunate family circumstances occurred with my father that preoccupied my time and all of the emotion seemed to stop. I later realized this was because my family issues served as a wonderful distraction. I was able to channel my energy away from my personal struggles and focus on my family.

As time went on, I felt an overwhelming urge to share my story, thinking that by telling others about my experience and helping them to cope with their own it would somehow help me deal with it myself. I spoke at several events by invitation of my commander and eventually was asked to be a guest speaker at the Non-Commissioned Officer Academy (NCOA) on base. I embraced the opportunity and felt the academy was an excellent medium to get my message across. I used my experience to deliver a lecture to the students on PTSD. It was a success with a tremendously positive reaction from the students. I felt I was making a difference by telling them how to avoid PTSD *as I had* by doing healthy things like exercise and not being ashamed to talk about their emotions and getting help... even though I never sought help and continued to struggle with my personal demons.

I vowed to run a half marathon in Rod's honor, feeling by doing so I would be able to gain some sort of closure. His memory haunted me every time I ran; I would see him and Jacko cheering me and waving each time I passed by.

I avoided things that would provoke emotions, such as news broadcasts and war movies. I found that giving the lectures was therapeutic in a sense, by finding the purpose in what I went through. I was seeing my experience, while it may have been unfortunate for me, was a way to help others. I held on to this idea and validation tightly, as if my life depended on it, but it still wasn't enough. I was still dancing around the depths of what was happening to me.

As I continued to train for the half marathon, that I titled "Rod's Race," I injured my left hip. I had been so accustomed to running on a rocky surface in Afghanistan that running on a pavement took its toll. I'd strained one of my adductor muscles, and instead of resting it and letting my body recover I continued to run. I would run 5-6 miles despite my pain; I had become an expert at ignoring both the emotional and physical signs that I was hurt. Eventually I got to the point where I couldn't even walk without a significant limp. I ended up in Physical Therapy for several months, with strict orders to rest. All of my training and conditioning melted away. Rod's Race was not even a possibility, I couldn't do it. Now I had failed myself emotionally and physically.

When I recovered from my injury, determined to accomplish my goal, I resumed running. My training; however, was short-lived. One morning in, April 2009, Greg and I were blessed with the news I was pregnant. I couldn't have been happier. It was the perfect time in our lives for a little one and I wanted to have a baby so badly. Throughout the pregnancy I continued to give my lectures and work in the clinic. Knowing I was going to be a mom served as yet another distraction to what I was feeling. It was no longer about me, but the little life I was bringing into the world and so all of my positive thoughts and energy went towards my unborn child. When I was twenty-two weeks along, at a routine OB appointment, it was discovered I was high risk due to an incompetent cervix. Given this was my first pregnancy, and due to the findings on the ultrasound, I was placed on modified bed-rest for the remainder of the pregnancy. This gave me a lot of time to think. I told myself it would be a great time to dive into the journal and start putting it into the book for my new little one, as I'd planned when I initially wrote it. Yet I couldn't open it; I would find myself staring at the book in silence while I sat at the computer. I would quickly find something else to do with my time, anything to avoid reliving any of the emotions.

Thankfully, the remainder of my pregnancy was uneventful and the baby was healthy. On the 4th of December 2009 I delivered beautiful little Ayla Lee Clark. I had no idea how overwhelming a mother's love truly is until I saw Ayla for the first time. The moment they laid her on my chest and I held her, the heart that had been broken so badly in Afghanistan filled with a new joy and love unlike anything I had ever experienced.

That joy was tarnished the night of the flashback. I knew I was not ok, and despite the new wonder in my life, my darkness was still there, and there was no hiding from it. From that moment I had several more episodes. We tried to watch a war movie that was incredibly realistic and took me right back to Afghanistan. Not thirty minutes into the film I felt my stomach turn and I began crying uncontrollably. My body became flushed and my heart was racing. I was having an anxiety attack. I ran from the living room and lay on my bed in the fetal position and shook with emotion.

Greg came after me and hugged me tightly, "It's ok sweetie, it's ok," he tried. I wished so desperately he was right. The memories began to manifest more frequently, my distractions were no longer effective, and I began to notice my haunting reminders impacting me more and more profoundly.

After my six weeks of maternity leave was over I returned to work. I felt a sense of purpose being back; having been away for several months it felt good to return to what I loved. At the same time, of course, it was bittersweet. I struggled every day having to leave Ayla at home. I wanted to be with her so badly, but I hoped work would help me to avoid the symptoms that continued to surface. I began to experience nightmares filled with gruesome details of crimes that were mainly focused towards women, waking me up at times in the middle of the night in fear. They were the type of dreams you wake up from, and it takes you a minute to realize it was actually just a dream. I eventually opened up and told a friend of mine, who was a psychologist. "You know Tracy, I should probably come over to the Mental Health clinic and talk to you," I confessed.

"Really? What's going on?" she asked.

"Oh. Well, you know it's really nothing, no big deal. I can get through it myself. I'm sure it's due to just having had Ayla," I said and quickly walked away. I could hear myself lying; I knew it was much more. I still wasn't comfortable with the idea of relying on someone else to help me deal with my issues. I'd already done so much by myself, there was no reason I couldn't handle this, right? I also continued to feel so incredibly alone. I told myself no one would be able to relate to what I was going through and because of this there was no way anyone could understand me or help in any way.

On an intellectual level, I knew better. I went to school and learned about this, and I was surrounded by peers who were fellow PAs, ARNPs (Nurse Practitioners), doctors, psychologists, psychiatrists, counselors, and social workers. Yet I was still insistent none of them would be of any help.

Two weeks after I returned to work, I was in the middle of my morning clinic when my new squadron commander came down to the clinic with a blue folder in her hand. As I was about to walk into my next exam room she pulled me aside.

"Hey, Jenn, I know you're busy, but do you have a minute to talk?" She had just arrived at the base several months before I was put on bed-rest and knew very little of who I was or what I'd been through.

"Yes ma'am, of course," I said and we walked into the hallway. She looked at me and shook her head.

"It's against my better judgment to do this, but I'm going to anyway. Jenn, you have a tasking…."

My heart stopped.

She continued, "It's for Afghanistan, for two-hundred seventy-nine days with three months of training prior to your departure."

Everything else she said was a blur. I broke out into a cold sweat and my heart was racing. My entire body felt like a giant hive.

"You won't be leaving until…."

"Excuse me ma'am-" I interrupted as I ran to the bathroom to dry heave. I tried to pull myself together but I was clearly shaken.

"Are you ok?" she asked.

"Yes ma'am, thank you," I replied, but inside my heart felt as if it was going to explode out of my chest. I couldn't even look at the folder. All I could think about was, *I can't go back there. I can't go back to that place.* I am ashamed to admit my reaction wasn't even due to the fact that I would be leaving my brand new baby. I didn't even get that far in my thought process. It was a response solely to "Afghanistan." She was understandably shocked by my reaction and didn't know what to do other than leave the folder with me, have some of my colleagues check on me, and let me continue with my clinic.

That moment was my turning point. I somehow found a way to make it through the rest of my clinic, but I honestly had to admit I was not there at all. I went through the motions, half-listening to what my patients were telling me, I couldn't stop seeing the blue folder in my head. I walked over to Mental Health Clinic later that day, because I couldn't pull myself out of the funk. I was so embarrassed to be seen, but I called my friend, Tera, a psychologist, who agreed I absolutely needed to be evaluated and would squeeze me in.

I was concerned about sitting in the waiting room; I couldn't bear running into one of my patients. "Tera, can you meet me at the back door?" I begged.

"Of course," she answered knowingly. As we sat in her office together I began to cry as I discussed what had happened earlier in the day. She had me fill out a questionnaire rating the severity of my symptoms. As she read through it she looked up and smiled and said, "Well, this is good Jenn. By the looks of it, it seems your symptoms are sub-clinical".

Great! I thought... and then we started talking. The more she asked, the more hesitant I became to discuss it. She began to dig into things I did not want to feel and I began to show clearly how upsetting it was.

She looked at me and said, "Jenn, you have really minimized your symptoms on paper, which is not surprising, but you are suffering much more than you admit, and my initial assessment of you is that you have chronic PTSD."

Hearing that was like getting hit in the gut.

"I have *what*? Are you kidding me? That can't be true Tera; it's nothing," I pleaded. *I am a provider*, I thought, *I don't get diagnosed with things like this, I help treat people with this, now you're saying that I have it*? She went on to explain the treatment course and what it consisted of. I would require exposure therapy, which would force me to face myself and all the feelings I had tucked away into a pretty little box in the very back of my closet of emotions, the feelings I wanted to forget about. I knew I had to make a decision right then and there. I could give up, let this new reality I was living in consume me and swallow the last bit of who I used to be, or I could begin my recovery, no matter how painful it may be. After much deliberation with myself, I chose recovery.

The tasking my poor new commander told me about was declined and I was deemed mentally unfit to return to Afghanistan in my current state. The treatment required me to meet with Tera every week, which was emotionally exhausting. I admitted finally to Greg what was going on, but still could not find a way to tell him my thoughts. He continued to give his support in the best ways he knew how, but still didn't understand what it all meant.

Fridays were my meetings with Tera and I would dread them every Thursday night. Greg would try to laugh with me the way we used to, but he would find me quiet and disconnected, especially on Thursdays, not knowing why or how to help. The therapy caused me to feel down the majority of the time, even angry for no particular reason. This was terribly uncomfortable for me; these feelings were so unfamiliar, because I'd been such a happy person before. I felt I was truly lost in a world of darkness that I couldn't pull myself out of, and every time I met with Tera she found a way to make that emotion surface and forced me to *feel* it.

She would ask me about certain instances, which I was able to talk about without issue because I had trained myself to do so in my lectures; but then she would dig, and ask me to describe things. She would ask me to talk about the details; the painful, horrible details that I never wanted to face again, down to how the air smelled. She took me back through all of it. I hated every minute of it. She kept making me remind myself who I had become. I was a person who felt hate and rage and I was so sad. I felt a sense of helplessness, certain I would never find my former self again.

Overwhelmed with such negativity I found myself going home and picking fights with Greg for no reason other than I wanted to fight. At work I would try to keep my office as stress-free as possible, with dimmed lights, and soft music, but it never failed. Someone was always coming in and complaining about things in their life or at the clinic and it sucked away any serenity and positivity I had gained and fed my negativity within.

I was about six months into my treatment, when I went to a conference in Atlanta over Memorial Day weekend. Greg, Ayla and Griffen spent the weekend with me but had to leave on Monday because Greg had to go back to work the following day. It was my first time away from Ayla and I was consumed with sadness the day they left. My sadness turned to anger with myself which then turned into disgust. I was up all night pacing and crying and screaming into my pillow because I was so angry with who I had become and how my world was forever changed.

My daughter would never know who her mother was before. She had to deal with this pathetic shell of who I used to be. After several hours of beating myself up mentally, I turned the light on in the bathroom and I looked in the mirror. My hair was all over the place, mascara streaming down my face, my eyes swollen and red from crying. I looked as ugly as I felt inside. I will never forget what I did next. I looked at myself, banged my head against the mirror and said out loud, "I fucking *hate* you" to the woman staring back at me, and I meant it from the depths of my soul. In that moment I felt as low as I'd ever felt in my life. I honestly could have cared less about what happened to me, and for the first time, I truly not only disliked myself; I loathed myself. I called Greg the next day and tried to explain to him what happened. It really shook me. I had never felt as bad as I did that night and didn't know what to do next.

He brushed it off and said, "Don't worry. It's ok. You'll be fine. No big deal." This had become his reaction to most of my emotional outcries during my therapy. I knew he meant well, but his

THE AFTERMATH

misunderstanding and minimizing what I was going through, made me feel even worse about myself. *If Greg doesn't think this is a big deal, why do I?*

When I returned from the conference I told Tera what happened and admitted I was really struggling. I denied feeling suicidal, despite my complete distain for myself, or homicidal (of course, the first questions every healthcare provider thinks to ask), but I didn't trust myself. I felt helpless. I agreed to see my primary care doctor, who prescribed me an anti-anxiety medication and an antidepressant.

I couldn't believe I had reached this point. I never thought I would ever be someone who would require those medications and here I was. As I held the antidepressant medication in my hand, I couldn't bring myself to take it. I held it for literally hours pacing the house trying to rationalize how I didn't need it. I thought of the many reassuring conversations I had previously with my own patients, struggling with the same stigma that I was.

I recalled my own words, "There is no shame in taking a medication for depression or anxiety if it is needed. It's just like needing to take something to help control high blood pressure or cholesterol."

It made so much sense to me from the outside looking in, but now it wasn't that easy. As I struggled with my personal medication dilemma I thought of Ayla, Griffen, and Greg. I couldn't keep going the way I was heading, especially after my breakdown. Finally, I submitted, and took the pill. I stayed on the medication for about six months and I do think it eventually helped, but not before I hit the lowest of the lows. My therapy continued to increase in intensity, and it showed. Eventually, Greg and I agreed he needed to come to a session with me and I was so nervous for him to see the vulnerable side of me. How would he react seeing me cry over the memories? He had told me time and time again how it wasn't a big deal. Now he would see how big I was making it. I just knew he was going to be so disappointed and ashamed of my weakness because I couldn't handle it by myself.

I couldn't have been more wrong. The appointment went surprisingly well, and all of my fears of him thinking I was weak or that my emotions were unjustified began to slowly fade away. He demonstrated no judgment, no disappointment. Instead he showed love and support and sorrow for his wife who clearly was hurting so much. He began to understand what I was going through and learned how to deal with it more effectively. I was able to explain how much damage his minimizing of everything was doing to me. He learned to key in on my emotions at home and when he saw me react to my triggers - the news, or a movie, or a sound - instead of watching me struggle and quickly turn off my emotion, as I'd done so frequently in the past, he insisted I face it. I would start to shut down, and he would pull me aside, sit me down at our kitchen table and hold my hands.

"Talk to me, Jenn. What are you feeling? Why? Tell me everything that this reminds you of," he would ask. I would try to dance around it as I always had, but he wised up to that and wouldn't let me.

"Tell me every detail, Jenn. It's okay. I am here," he said. His acceptance began to pull me through it.

I still had a long way to go. I will never forget the turning point. I went to my session one day and I was clearly upset and exhausted from everything we had been through. I sat in the chair with my legs crossed and she noticed that I was pumping my leg very intentionally, yet I didn't realize it.

"What's that about?" she pointed to my leg.

"What?" I looked down and saw my leg. I didn't have an answer. I was so filled with all of the negative emotions I was being forced to face that they had consumed me.

Tera looked at me and said, "Jenn, you will get through this."

I looked at her and through my tears I said, "I really don't know if I will."

"I can see you're really in the eye of the storm, just hang in there with me."

"Uh-huh," I replied. I couldn't even look her in the eye. I didn't believe there was anything else I could do. I felt defeated. I went home that day and Greg and I got into an argument for something so insignificant I can't even recall it. But, I *needed* to be angry, so I

THE AFTERMATH

provoked him to fight with me.

He had Ayla in his arms, and as we argued, my voice got louder and so did his. Ayla began to cry in fear as she watched her mother lose control. I found myself filled with rage and I picked up her bottle and threw it as hard as I could against the wall causing milk to go everywhere and stormed out of the house screaming at him as I got into my car. I drove and drove and eventually parked in a place on base where I was out of the view of anyone who may have driven by. I turned the car off and screamed at the top of my lungs, "WHY? WHY GOD? WHY?" over and over again. I screamed and I hit my steering wheel as hard as I could. I needed to know why God let these things happen in this world. Why did innocent people hurt and suffer and die in the ways that I was exposed to? What was the purpose in this? Why did I have to witness it? Why did God let my innocence die with them? Why was I no longer that bubbly, optimistic, lighthearted and trusting person I was before I went to that place? Where was that fire inside of me? I used to laugh, I used to make a difference, I used to *care*. I was none of those things anymore.

Who was I? I hated. I had never felt true hatred before in my life and now I was living with it every day. I was filled with *anger* and *rage* and *negativity*. I screamed and screamed and screamed and cried and cried until I was physically exhausted. I looked down at my clock; thirty minutes had passed. I turned the car on and drove to the beach. I walked down the boardwalk and saw there was a wedding about to start just a few short yards away from me as I walked down to the shore. I sat in the sand with my toes in the water and listened to the waves crashing against the shoreline. I watched the happy couple celebrate their love with their friends and families, and it reminded me of my own wedding day.

I smiled as I reminisced on the best day of my life. Everything was perfect. It was such a celebration of the love and the friendship I had with my Gerg. My Gerg...the beautiful man that I just picked a fight with and hurt for no reason. I pulled my knees up to my chest and rested my chin on my knees as I sat in silence. My tears were all dried out from the car, but I felt the lump in my throat forming as I thought of Greg. I had neglected to realize how much my pain was hurting him.

So many people stand together and take those vows, just as the couple on the beach was doing, just as Greg and I did, yet less than half of them actually stay together. I knew in that moment I had to pull through this not only for myself, but for my husband, and for our family. I looked out to the water and thought of my childhood. In my early years we lived in California and almost every day my mother took my sister and me to the beach to play in the water and explore. That was the very beginning of my life and here I sat, a mother myself, desperately searching for hope and purpose.

I closed my eyes and I felt the breeze in my hair and the water on my toes. I ran my fingers through the sand and when I opened my eyes I looked at the beautiful turquoise water in front of me and in that moment, I regained hope. For the first time in almost a year of therapy I realized I would get through it. I didn't doubt; I knew. I accepted on that day I was not the same person as I was before I left, but I was still *me*, and I could pull through this.

From that day on the beach forward, I began to appreciate the road to recovery. I made a decision that it was time I readdress the journal. I found the strength to sit down and put it into a document as I'd intended so long ago. After several months, it was complete and ready to read. Greg was the first person I asked to read it. I was so nervous again. I didn't want him to think I wasn't strong enough to deal with the situations I'd faced; and once he read it, he would have so much more of the details I was not able to share otherwise.

Tera agreed it was the absolute right thing to do, so I gave it to him. He read it in several days, and admitted he couldn't put it down. Each time he got to a difficult experience, instead of being ashamed of me as I had feared, he held me... so tightly... and he cried with me. Sometimes, he even sobbed. He had *no* idea the extent of what had happened and he was so touched I was able to finally share it with him. When he finished it, he didn't tell me I should have done anything differently. Instead he told me he was proud of me, and proud to be my husband. Having him read it and see his heartfelt reaction did more for me than I could've imagined. It gave me the strength to move on, and it became the beginning the next chapter in my life.

CHAPTER 45

Back to Center

I returned to the NCOA (Non-Commissioned Officer Academy) with a whole new approach to my lecture, and spoke from the heart about my personal struggles with PTSD and how I was getting through it. I shared the journal with my family and then I began to share it with friends. Each time it was read the feedback was overwhelming. People were getting something from my experience. The lectures were impacting people in such effective ways. My pain, my struggle began to have a purpose. I became more and more receptive to people as they told me their own stories after hearing mine.

The story began to reach people in a much greater way. People who were struggling from experiences outside of military deployments - life in general - were finding the strength they needed to face their own darkness within. They were moved to the point they realized it was time to get help and that it was ok. The more this happened, the bigger my experience became and I began to realize it was much bigger than me.

It wasn't about me anymore. It was about reaching out to people and touching their lives with the hand of understanding and reassurance they needed to move on. I became the voice some couldn't be, that they needed. As a woman, I realized how unique and unspoken my perspective was, and as I watched more and more of my fellow female active duty friends suffer in silence I saw the importance of my speaking out. As a woman, living in a man's military world, it was even harder to show any emotion because of the infamous stereotype, "It's because you're a woman." I had to fight harder and prove myself my entire military career. I had to show I could handle the same things my male counterparts could; therefore, I couldn't show weakness or vulnerability.

Realizing this in myself, I understood my reactions and assumptions to Greg's response to my situation. I soon realized my fellow female service members shared the same burdens I was carrying. I knew I needed to be that voice, for them. This empowered me to continue with this calling. I began to feel my empty heart slowly start to fill again, with each person I was able to reach. The more time passed, the more important it became. I continued to let people read the journal and each one who did stated that they felt I needed to do something with it...yet I couldn't bring myself to do it. I wasn't ready. My marriage continued to grow, and my husband became my rock in more ways than I ever could have hoped for. I was so thankful that he decided to hang in there with me. He didn't give up and neither did I.

I began running again, and so did Greg. He reminded me of the promise I'd once made to run Rod's Race and said he would run it with me; side by side. We began to train together several days a week and eventually signed up for a race. We paid and registered; the commitment was made. We were doing the half marathon. We also recruited several friends to run it with us, including Tera. I knew I had to do it, for Rod. As time went on the race day grew closer and closer. I found myself becoming more and more emotional about it. Greg and I had shirts made saying, "Rod's Race" on the front, with our dedication to Greg Rodriguez on the back.

Despite my multiple failed attempts to do it in the past, I knew this was it. On the day of the race I was so overcome with emotion. I made sure "Simple Man" was on my playlist on my iPod that day, as I wanted the whole 13.1 miles to be in honor of Rod, our fallen hero. As I ran each mile, I thought of all the good memories I had of my friend. Several times throughout the race we had people give us pats on the shoulder as they read our shirts and people yelled from the sidelines, "Let's go Rod's Race!" as we passed. It was incredible. As we completed mile eleven I hit a peak of emotion and during the entire final mile I had tears streaming down my face as I honored my friend. When we crossed the finish line, Greg and I held hands and I pointed up to the sky with my free hand as I said, "This is all for you Rod!" It was a moment that words cannot begin to describe. I needed desperately to accomplish that for him and it was incredible that Greg was able to complete it with me. It was a giant step towards closure for me.

I eventually pinned on Captain, and each day got easier, but I knew the military chapter in my life was ending. I needed to move on. I was now a mother, and I recognized that though my heart was once very much involved in the military, it was no longer. I needed to let go of my past in order to move forward with my future. Saying goodbye to the life I'd known my entire adulthood was a very scary thing, but after ten years seven months and three days of service, I took off my uniform and unlaced my boots for the last time. I cannot begin to express the amount of pride I have in my heart for my time in the Air Force and the experiences I had, and I admire those who give so much more than I ever could.

During my own journey to recovery, I heard news of another team member who also struggled greatly with the realities of the experience in Afghanistan. Remember the Australian bomb dog Sarbi? She'd gone missing after the battle on September 2nd. Apparently they never gave up hope in finding her and returned to the firebase multiple times in hopes to bring her home. After fourteen months, she was finally recovered by an American soldier who noticed her walking with a local Afghan. She was unharmed and healthy and eventually was returned to Australia and her handler, who was one of the soldiers wounded in the attack. She later received the Purple Cross, Australia's most prestigious animal bravery award, from the RSPCA. This award recognizes animals for outstanding service to humans, particularly if they risk their own life or safety to save a person from injury or death.

There has even been a book written to tell the amazing story of her survival.

When I heard of her story, I also learned that one of the Aussie soldiers became the first recipient of the Victoria Cross for Australia for his actions during the battle. This is the highest award in the Australian Honors System. I was honored to have been in the company of both of these war heroes, and it warmed my heart to know Sarbi made it home. I felt while the road for our individual journeys was bumpy and seemed never-ending for us both, we each eventually found our way back.

After I separated from the Air Force, Greg and I agreed we would both pursue our dream jobs and whoever got their job first would determine where we ended up next. Greg had a friend at his current job he talked to frequently about me, and she knew I was a PA. She told Greg about a Vascular Surgeon named Bud Shuler in Panama City that I had to meet. "Greg, it's one of those things I feel is just meant to be," she said. She helped coordinate an interview and when I met him I knew instantly it was a fit. We spent two hours in the interview talking about making a difference for our patients. I was offered the job on the spot, and I couldn't have been more excited. I couldn't wait to get home and share the news with Greg. He saw the excitement in my eyes and it brought him to tears.

"Jenn, I haven't seen you *happy* like this in such a long time. You have that spark again," he said, and he was right. I was truly happy about where the future was taking me in my career path. The very next day, he was offered a position in Washington D.C. that was essentially *his* dream job. When he told me the news I said, "What are we going to do?"

"That's easy, Jenn. We stay. This job, the practice, and the people you are about to work with has lit that fire again in you. It's a no brainer; this is where we are supposed to be." So we officially planted our roots and I became a member of Vascular Associates.

Time went on and I continued to heal. The Special Forces group I was with ended up moving down to Florida and I was able to reunite with Hal. We sat down to dinner one night and I had the opportunity to introduce my husband to the man who took such great care of me and Becky while we were away. Seeing them together was amazing. They immediately connected, and hugged like they were long lost friends.

"So, you're Hal? Huh, Funny, I thought you were taller," Greg said.

"Well that's okay. I thought you were fatter," Hal replied, and they were instant friends. Watching them sit and talk and get to know each other was an incredible moment for me. I had an amazing bond with Hal after our experience in Afghanistan; I would walk through fire for him. I truly loved him as a brother and I was so fortunate to have a husband who completely understood and respected our friendship.

"Hey man, listen, I can't thank you enough for watching over her," Greg said with tears in his eyes.

"Greg, thank you for allowing her to be a part of our team. I don't want to think about how that deployment would have gone without her," Hal said. Hearing him say that to my husband offered validation to me for what I did; I'd always wondered if I did enough. As dinner came to an end, and we said our goodbyes for the evening, I felt such gratitude for the friendship I had and that Greg was forming with Hal. We're still very close and we spend time with each other's families as often as we can.

I still needed closure with Afghanistan and Greg knew it. He knew exactly what needed to happen, so he took it upon himself to make it so. He called Bud and arranged for me to have time off and surprised me with a trip to Arlington National Cemetery. It was time for me to say goodbye to an old friend. I couldn't find the words to tell him how touched I was that he had gone to such trouble for me.

I was so nervous, my heart started pounding as soon as we got in the car the morning we visited Arlington. I couldn't stop thinking about the last time I saw Rod. As we walked into the Visitor Center a lump formed in my throat and I was overwhelmed with emotion. As I stood in front of the kiosk, that would give us the location of Rod's gravesite, I reached out to enter his name and my hand was shaking so badly I couldn't steady it long enough to push the keys. Greg took over, and as the paper printed he grabbed my hand and squeezed it tightly.

"You ready to do this sweetie?" he asked.

"As I'll ever be," I managed, and we walked out the door and started on our long journey to his grave. I was speechless with solace as we walked through the sea of white tombstones around us. It was breathtaking. So many souls had paid the ultimate sacrifice. We were surrounded by thousands, upon thousands of heroes. It was such a significant moment; it put so much into perspective. The walk to Section 60 seemed never-ending, which was fine by me. I didn't know if I could do it, face the memory head on. I thought of the moments I shared with Rod, and how they were such a small part of his life, but they were so important in mine. I was honored to have known him and proud to have served next to him. I thought of the last morning I spoke to him and the last time I saw his body.

I felt nauseous. My stomach was in knots. *Ugh. What do I say to him? How do I say goodbye? Am I going to be able to do this?*

"Jenn.....Jenn? We're here," Greg said.

"Huh?" I looked up and realized we had stopped walking and we were standing in Section 60 and next to his row.

"He should be about halfway down," Greg pointed, "Do you want me to come with you?"

"Um...no. I'm ok," I said. I took a deep breath and started walking down the row. My legs felt like a ton of bricks as I made my way towards him. I looked at the names and the birthdates on the headstones that I walked by. So many young soldiers, most were younger than I was. I looked at the dates that they were killed, all around that same time period as Rod. I walked by the flowers, the gifts that family and friends left for their fallen heroes. Many left pictures and letters and it was heartbreaking.

And just like that, I was standing in front of his grave. I saw his name and instantly started to sob. I knelt down and put my hand on his headstone and just wept. I was surprised by the emotion that came to the surface and how quickly I was overcome with it. I had learned through my therapy to let it happen, so I did. I let all of the tears flow, all of the pain and sadness needed to come out. I wanted to say something, but for several moments there were no words. I brought the medal I was awarded for my deployment and my squadron coin to leave with him. I held them so tightly in my hands as I knelt and cried for my friend. I remembered the day with our salad and our silly conversations. I remembered how he worked so hard with Jacko, and the nights he was at the track while I ran. I remembered the last words we spoke, and I remembered seeing him lying there in the clinic, so peacefully in a pool of blood. I remembered having to step over him, and watching his body being loaded into a bag and onto the helicopter.

"My dear friend, I don't know what to say to you right now. I just....want...I just *need* to say I am sorry. I am so sorry. Not a day goes by that I am not grateful for the few moments we spent together. I am honored. You are a hero; you are my hero. Thank you…Thank you….Thank you….Thank you."

I must have said those two words ten to fifteen times, but it was all that could come out. I looked down at my medal and my coin and I squeezed them in my hands one last time, and I placed them in front of his grave. I stood and looked up and saw my dear husband standing with tear-filled eyes several feet away. I waved him over and hugged him tightly. We stood together in silence in front of Rod for several minutes. I was finally ready.

"Goodbye my friend," I said and I turned and walked away. As we walked, I could feel the weight had been lifted from my heart. I had no idea how much I needed that moment. I felt such a sense of closure, knowing that my last memory of seeing Rod was no longer that terrible day. I felt after that moment I could easily return to his grave and not be scared or nervous about my emotion, but for a visit that would be a peaceful reunion with a memory of a friend. It was a huge day for my recovery.

September 2nd was always a hard day for me. The first anniversary of that fateful day I literally couldn't take it and had to leave work. The next year was a little easier, but still very emotional, which took a lot out of me. The third anniversary, in 2011, took a turn for the better. I'd been feeling rather sick for several weeks and had taken a home pregnancy test the night before and it was positive. The morning of the 2nd I decided to make an appointment and have an official test. On the way to the clinic I began to cry as I recalled the events of the fateful day in 2008. I arrived at the clinic, and after submitting a blood sample, it was official. I was having another baby. I could now associate September 2nd with a beautiful moment in my life, and that was so important.

We brought Dylan Patrick into the world in April 2012, completing our beautiful family. He is such a strong little man with a huge heart and a kind soul. I can't begin to express how grateful I am that my children are the beautiful little people that they are.

I feel my life is filled with so many blessings. I am overwhelmed with gratitude for the Divine guidance I have been able to key into and recognize throughout my life. This perspective has been the way I have found purpose in my misfortunes. I continue to live every moment to its fullest and appreciate every blessing in my life with a humility that I never knew prior to my experience. I have finally accepted I did change, and while I left my innocence over there, I brought back a perspective that made me a better, more impactful person.

I was able to reignite that fire inside eventually. I did so by accepting the reality I have very little control over what is meant to be, and by serving others, I was able to find reason in misfortune. I have embraced motherhood, and my family, and have made them my top priority. I think of the people I was with on an almost daily basis. I have realized finally how *big* the deployment really was. This took me a long time to do. I minimized it for so long, but have now allowed myself to *feel* the emotions I never felt while I was there. Rod and Travis are forever in my heart and I take every opportunity to tell people I meet about the heroes they were. I am truly blessed to have such wonderful family and friends.

People often ask me, "If you had it to do over again, would you?"

I tell them without hesitation, "Absolutely." Afghanistan was filled with some of the worst moments of my life, but also many of the best moments of my military career. The experience has helped me become the person I am today and for that I am forever grateful. It has turned into a story of hope and inspiration. I have accepted that while I witnessed horrific things, and I hit a place that was the lowest of the lows, it all came down to a decision that only I could make. I could do nothing and be consumed by my darkness within or I could accept what happened and move on, no matter how painful the road to recovery may be. I chose to come through that darkness and into the light. My road was long and painful, filled with unexpected turns and detours, but by the graceful guidance of God I eventually found my way back to center.